ĀSANAS

SWAMI KUVALAYANANDA

KAIVALYADHAMA
Swami Kuvalayananda Marg,
Lonavla (410 403), Maharashtra, INDIA

First published	1933
Second Edition	1937
Third Edition	1949
Fourth Edition	1964
Fifth Edition	1971
Sixth Edition	1977
Seventh Edition	1993
Eighth Edition	2012
Ninth Edition	2017
Tenth Edition	2024

ISBN 81-89485-04-0

RS : 300/-

Published by:
Kaivalyadhama,
Swami Kuvalayananda Marg,
Lonavla, Dist. Pune – 410 403,
(M.S.) INDIA

ACE Enterprises
137/A, Paud Rosd,
Madhuraj Nagar, C1/6,
Kothrud, Pune - 411038,
Maharashtra (INDIA)
Tel. : 020 - 67678392

Yoga has a complete message for humanity.
It has a message for the human body.
It has a message for the human mind
and it has also a message for the human soul.
Will intelligent and capable youth come forth
to carry this message to every individual,
not only in India but also in every other part of the world?

- Swami Kuvalayananda

CONTENT

01 Human Body

p.1-38

02 Preparing Oneself for Āsanas

p. 39-47

Yoga has a complete message for humanity. It has a message for the human mind. And it has also a message for the human soul.

03 Meditative Poses

p. 48-62

PREFACE TO THE PRESENT REVISED EDITION 2017

मूकं करोति वाचालं पङ्गुं लङ्घयते गिरिम् ।
यत्कृपा तमहं वन्दे परमानन्दमाधवम् ॥

(Reverence to Mādhava, the Supreme Bliss! Blessed by Him the dumb shall grow eloquent and the lame shall stride across a mountain).

We feel immense satisfaction in presenting this new revised edition 2017 of the handbook on Asanas to the lovers of Yoga. Though the content of the edition is similar to the earlier editions there are various newly added relevant themes such as The Rationale of Yogic Poses worked by Swamiji himself as early as July 1926. This rationale is in terms of Scientific and Traditional understanding of Āsanas which underlies this text on Āsanas. We have also included a short biography of Swamiji and information on the institutional activities that have emerged under the guidelines and inspirations from him.

The text is presented with several improvised illustrations based on the actual text which were missing in the earlier editions. The readers will find these illustrations in the very body of the text instead of at the end of the text in the form of Appendix. This will facilitate the understanding of āsanas along with the pictures/ anatomical illustrations etc. specially designed for the purpose. The Appendices though contain the similar matter as available in earlier editions they are rendered in this new edition with improvised and Sadhana friendly presentation techniques providing totally a new look to the text.

We have also overcome various shortcomings that we came across in the earlier editions making the text more and more accurate and error proof.

Our thanks are due to Sri Subodh Tiwari, CEO, for conceiving such a presentation of the text. We thank Sri O.P. Tiwari for his encouragement, guidance and appreciation of the work. Towards the preparation of this edition Sri R.K. Bodhe, Assistant Director of Philosophico-Literary Research Department of Kaivalyadhama (In charge) and Sasinee Panyarat and Ida Blazek-the internees working in the department - and the Departmental Staff we are thankful for their contribution in this regard.

Mr. Bernard Britto owes our thanks for the work of coordination towards the publication of this edition.

We hope that the present edition will be appreciated by the lovers of Yoga atlarge.

Om Shanti Shanti Shanti.

SWAMI MAHESHNANDA
Kaivalyadhama, Lonavla
28-12-2017

PREFACE

मूकं करोति वाचालं पङ्गुं लङ्घयते गिरिम् ।
यत्कृपा तमहं वन्दे परमानन्दमाधवम् ॥

(Reverence to Mādhava, the Supreme Bliss!
Blessed by Him the dumb shall grow eloquent
and the lame shall stride across a mountain).

We have great pleasure in presenting this handbook of Āsanas to the public. It gives detailed description of the technique of nearly every Āsanas that has physical or a spiritual value. With a view to making the description more intelligible each Āsanas has been fully illustrated. In this way the handbook has become a reliable and competent guide to the students of Yoga who wish to follow the Short, Full and Easy Courses of Yogic Physical Culture framed by the Kaivalyadhama. In order to cover the whole field of physical culture included in the Short, Full and Easy Courses, Viparīta Karaṇī, Yoga-Mudrā, Uḍḍiyāna and Nauli have been discussed in this handbook, although, technically speaking, they are not Āsanas. If a reader students our handbook of Prāṇāyāma along with this handbook, he will know almost everything that worth knowing for a practical student of Yogic Physical Culture.

We haven't left out of consideration the claims of a spiritual culturist either. Preparing Oneself for Āsanas and Meditative Poses—these two Chapters of this handbook, coupled with our discussion on the spiritual aspect of Prāṇāyāma contained in the other handbook of Popular Yoga, are quite sufficient to enable an Ādhyātmic student of Yoga to make a fair beginning.

At the end every exercise the physical and therapeutic advantages have been very briefly stated. We have done this with a view to inculcate the importance of the different exercises upon the minds of our readers. Readers of Popular Yoga are to be warned, however, not to practice Yogic Therapy on the strength of the knowledge thus obtained, because half knowledge is a dangerous thing and the knowledge of Yogic Therapy is no exception to the general rule. We have also to draw our readers particular attention to the caution given in this book at various places.

This handbook is intended to be a practical guide for Yogic poses. As such, it does not contain any extensive theoretical discussions on the different exercises included in it. This fact should not, however, be taken to mean that the readers of this handbook will have no knowledge of the anatomy and physiology of Āsanas. The first and the last chapters will surely give our readers a fairly good idea regarding all the functional advantages of the Āsanas along sound scientific lines. But, after all, the treatment of the subject is from the practical rather than from the theoretical point of view. The theoretical aspect of the culture and therapy of Āsanas will be more extensively dealt with in another volume. The two put together will give almost everything that an average student of Yogic poses is expected to know both practically and theoretically.

Those who wish to have a thorough knowledge of the theory and practice of Yogic poses must read Yoga Mīmāṁsā where pages after pages are devoted to the discussion of the physiological and therapeutical values of Āsanas, everywhere the discussion being based on original laboratory experiments. The two volumes of Popular Yoga are intended only for those who have almost nothing but practical interest in Yoga.

Even before bringing out this handbook of Āsanas we have published a Chart of Yogic Poses supplied with a pamphlet that tersely explains the technique of each Āsana. In this connection also we want to bring the following fact to the notice of our readers. Just as this handbook is in substitute for Yoga Mīmāṁsā, the Chart is no substitute for this handbook. The technique given with the Chart is, indeed, correct and sufficient to direct a practical student of Yoga. But the treatment is so terse and so bereft of any anatomical, physiological or therapeutical considerations, that it is nothing when compared with the material presented in this handbook.

The technique of the Yogic exercises described in Yoga Mīmāṁsā, this handbook or the Chart is directly taken from old Yogic textbooks in Saṅskṛit and ancient Yogic traditions, with only very few minor changes. This technique should be faithfully followed in the individual practice of these exercises. The physiological and therapeutical advantages claimed for these exercises are the results of this technique.

Our cordial thanks are due to the brother Ashramites for their affectionate co-operation.

This is the fourth edition of the popular handbook which was not available for a long time. We hope that it will receive the same wide patronage that was received by it earlier.

We have been engaged in the editorial work for over two decades. In spite of our many shortcomings, some of them very serious, we have been consistently treated with great indulgence by the public. We crave the same indulgence hereafter.

Yoga has a complete message for humanity. It has a message for the human body. It has a message for the human mind. And it has also a message for the human soul. Will intelligent and capable youths come forth to carry this message to every individual, not only in India but also in every other part of the world?

KUVALAYANANDA
Lonavla
2-10-64.

SYSTEM OF TRANSLITERATION FOLLOWED IN THIS HANDBOOK

ॐ (ओम्)	'aum'	pronounce	'au'	like	'o'	in	'home'
अ	'a'	"	'a'	"	'u'	"	'but'
आ	'ā'	घ्	'gh'		ध्		'dh'
इ	'i'	ङ्	'ṅ'		न्		'n'
ई	'ī'	च्	'c'		प्		'p'
उ	'u'	छ्	'ch'		फ्		'ph'
ऊ	'ū'	ज्	'j'		ब्		'b'
ऋ	'ṛ'	झ्	'jh'		भ्		'bh'
ॠ	'ṝ'	ञ्	'ñ'		म्		'm'
ऌ	'lṛ'	ट्	'ṭ'		य्		'y'
ए	'e'	ठ्	'ṭh'		र्		'r'
ऐ	'ai'	ड्	'ḍ'		ल्		'l'
ओ	'o'	ढ्	'ḍh'		व्		'v'
औ	'au'	ण्	'ṇ'		श्		'ś'
क्	'k'	त्	't'		ष्		'ṣ'
ख्	'kh'	थ्	'th'		स्		's'
ग्	'g'	द्	'd'		ह		'h'

'l' a dento-lingual pronounced with a little rounding of lips.

Nasalized म् as in संयम - ṃ Nasalized म् as in संलग्न - ṃ

" " " " संवाद - m " " " संहिता - m;

Nasalized न् as in मीमांसा - ṅ; Visarga - ḥ

LIST OF ILLUSTRATION

1
HUMAN BODY

Broadly speaking the human body consists of two central parts called the trunk and the head. Attached to the trunk at its upper corners are the arms and its lower corners are the legs. The arms are termed the upper extremities and the legs are known as lower extremities. Bones are the hardest parts of the human body and form the framework of the physical structure. This framework of bones is called the skeleton and supports the softer parts of the body such as muscles which are attached to it. It also offers effective protection to some other parts of the human organism. For instance, some of the bones are arranged in such a way that they give wonderful protection to the brain, the spinal cord, the heart and the lungs. The brain is held securely in the bony case of the skull and the spinal cord is safely lodged in the hollow of the backbone. Similarly the heart and the lungs are located within the cage of the ribs. A very important group of organs such as the stomach, the intestines, the liver, the spleen, the pancreas, and the kidneys, is situated inside the belly. These organs are ably protected there by means of very strong muscles that go to form the walls of the belly and are attached to the bones at the two ends. Thus we find that the bony framework of the human body protects directly or indirectly all the organs of vital importance and also supports human flesh in the form of muscles in which it is clothed. These muscles, however, would have given a very uneven surface to the human body had it not been for the fat which fill up the depressions in the muscles and gives a rounded appearance to the different parts. What little roughness would still be persisting, is smoothed down by the skin forming the outermost coat of the human body.

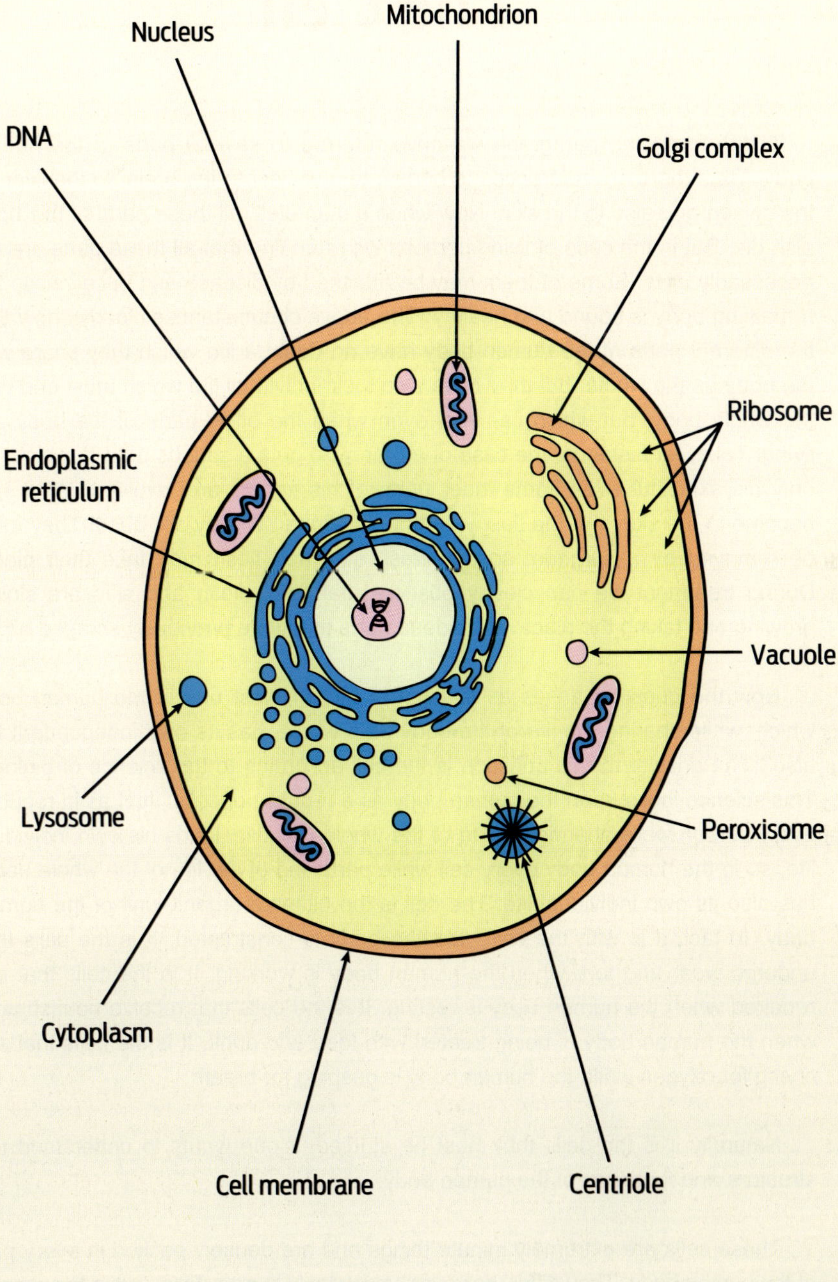
Mitochondrion
Nucleus
DNA
Golgi complex
Ribosome
Endoplasmic reticulum
Vacuole
Lysosome
Peroxisome
Cytoplasm
Cell membrane
Centriole

FIG.1

The Cell

In the foregoing paragraph we have referred to several parts of the human body. Thus there are references to bones, to muscles, to the brain, to the liver, to the spleen and also to the skin. Now when a man dies, all these parts of this body also die. But in the case of living persons we often find that all these parts are not necessarily alive. Some of them may be attacked by disease and decay while the remaining body is sound and healthy. The above circumstances clearly show that the different parts of the human body have no doubt a life which they share with the body as the whole, but they have also their individual life which must end with the whole body, but which can end even when the other parts of the body are living. Take, for instance, the case of a man who gets a serious burn in which not only his skin, but even some inner parts of his fingers are involved. What has become to the skin and the fleshy parts of his fingers? They are dead! They must be removed by a surgeon, so that fresh skin and flesh may take their place. During treatment we can clearly observe that living flesh and skin are slowly growing and taking the place of the dead parts that were previously scraped off.

Now the question arises as to what is the smallest unit in the human body which, while sharing the life of the body as a whole, has its own independent life also? The answer to this question is the cell according to the science of biology. This science looks upon the human body as a republic of cells. Just as in republic every person while sharing the life of the whole republic, leads his own individual life, so in the human body every cell while partaking of the life of the whole body, has also its own individual life. The cell is the ultimate organic unit of the human body. In fact, it is with the cells that the body is constructed. It is the cells that undergo wear and tear when the human body is working. It is the cells that are repaired when the human body is resting. It is the cells that receive nourishment when the human body is being treated with food and drink. It is the cells that are crying for oxygen while the human body is gasping for breath.

Naturally it is the cells that must be studied, if one wants to understand the structure and functions of the human body.

These cells are extremely minute things and are densely packed in every part of the human body. They differ, however, very widely in size. Thus within the space of a cubic millimeter we can hold several millions of them, if they are of the smallest variety; but within the same space we cannot hold more than a thousand, if they happen to be of the biggest size. It is calculated that we carry more than 5,000,000 of these cells in a tiny drop of blood, that is only as big as one cubic millimeter.

What is the stuff of which the cells are made? They are made of a substance that is known as protoplasm. It resembles the white of an egg and is considered by the biologist to be the physical basis of all life. Biologists have come to the conclusion that there is no life apart from protoplasm. It is because of this protoplasm the cell can become an independent organic unit so much so that it can live, it can take nourishment, it can grow and it can even reproduce its own kind.

The process of cell-reproduction is very interesting. Each cell has a highly specialized central part called the nucleus. The nucleus is as it were the very soul of the cell. So when the process of reproduction starts, the nucleus first divides itself into two. The two parts begin to work independently and develop themselves into two full-fledged cells. When the development is completed, they separate themselves into two cells either of which can in its turn, become a mother and reproduce two cells from itself. This process of cell-multiplication can best be observed in rapidly healing wound where a large number of these cells is reproduced every day.

Although all cells are uniformly made of protoplasm, they mutually differ in form according to the form of the organs to which they belong. For instance, muscles-cells are spindle-shaped, but gland-cells are cubical in form.

Several cells combine to form what are called tissues in anatomy. Broadly speaking, in some of the tissues of the human body the original cells are changed into fibers. Thus the fibers of the nerves and of the skeletal muscles are only modifications of the cells. Every tissue has got not only its distinctive form but also its specialized function to perform. Organs all over the body are made of these tissues, every one of which is characterized by the functional activity of the organs to which it belongs. The activity of the muscles is characterized by their contraction, so every muscular tissue will be found to contract when stimulated to action. If a tissue belongs to a gland, it will be found to secrete juices when active. Similarly a nervous tissue will be found capable of transmitting impulses.

Thus we have seen that the ultimate organic units of the human body are cells. These cells combine themselves into tissues each of which has its characteristic form and function according to the form and function of the organs to which it belongs. But what is it that enables the cells to live and function? As these cells work, they must undergo wear and tear. What is it that enables them to repair themselves? The answer of this question is nourishment. Every one of these cells is constantly being supplied with nourishment in the form of oxygen, water, proteins, fats, sugars and salts. This nourishment is derived from the air we breathe, the liquids we drink, and the solids we eat. Out of this nourishment cells are able to manufacture protoplasm which enables them to live and function and even to multiply.

We shall now proceed first to study the arrangements made in the human body for carrying its nourishment to every cell and then to see how the nourishing elements are prepared out of the food and drink that we take by the mouth, and the air we take in by the nose. But even before we do this, we shall take a short notice of the bones and muscles that go to form the bulk of the human body.

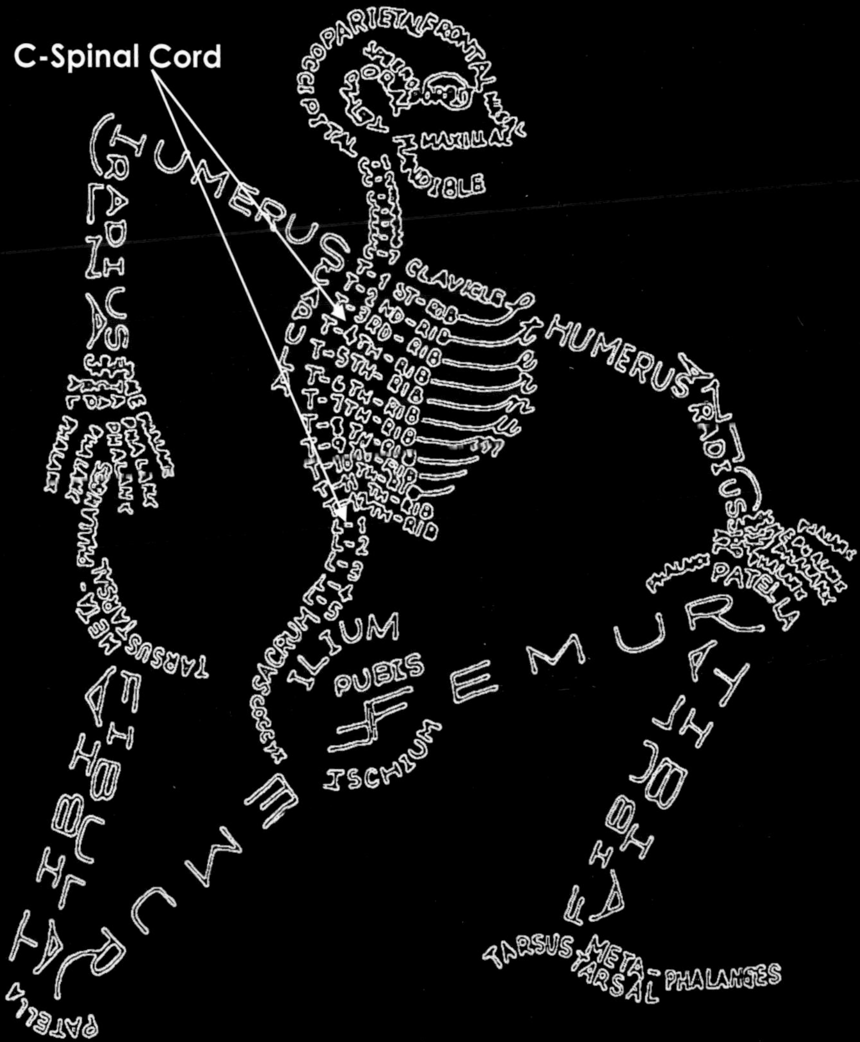
C-Spinal Cord
PARIETAL
FRONTAL
MAXILLA
MANDIBLE
CLAVICLE
HUMERUS
HUMERUS
RADIUS
RADIUS
ULNA
ILIUM
PUBIS
ISCHIUM
SACRUM
FEMUR
FEMUR
TIBIA
FIBULA
TIBIA
FIBULA
PATELLA
PATELLA
TARSUS
TARSUS META-TARSAL PHALANGES

FIG.2

Bone

There are about two hundred bones in human adult. As stated in the introduction of this chapter they form the framework of the human body and support the softer parts thereof. Fig. 2 illustrates the human skeleton. This illustration will make it clear that not only our trunk, legs and arms , but even our toes and fingers have these hard bones running through them. Bones are joined together by means of joints most of which allow them movements within particular limits. These movements are brought about by muscles which connect the two bones joined together. In order that the movements of the joints may be smooth, not only soft pads of cartilages are inserted between the joining bones, but also a sort of lubrication is made available there in the form of secretions.

The most wonderful structure containing a series of joints is the backbone or the vertebral column. This column originally consists of 33 separate pieces of bones, each piece called a vertebra. In Fig. 2 they are marked with Roman figures. It will be discovered that they are only 26 because several of them have become fused together as they do in the case of an adult. The first seven vertebrae are situated in the neck and hence are called cervical, from cervix: the neck. The twelve that follow are located in the region of the back and are, therefore, named dorsal. The next five are called lumber because they support the loins. Below these is the sacrum, originally consisting of five bones but afterwards of one continuous piece, the separate parts being united. The last piece is the coccyx formed by four rudimentary vertebrae.

These vertebrae are arranged one on the top of the other, so that every one of them fits in with the one immediately above it and also with the one immediately below it through partially movable joints. Between these vertebrae soft bony substances are placed to serve as cushions. They are called cartilages, and allow free movement to the vertebrae. Strong fibrous bands called ligaments bind together these 26 separate pieces of the vertebral column. Each vertebrae has a hollow ring inside it. The column is so arranged as to keep these rings, one above the other, forming a canal for the spinal cord to lie in. It is, therefore, called the spinal canal. In Fig. 2 this canal is indicated by C.

Very strong muscles surround this vertebral column and enable it to move in almost all directions. Thus it can bend backwards and forwards, to the right and to the left, so also it can have considerable right and left twists. 31 pairs of spinal nerves exit through the spaces left between every two adjoining vertebrae and spread themselves to the different parts of the body.

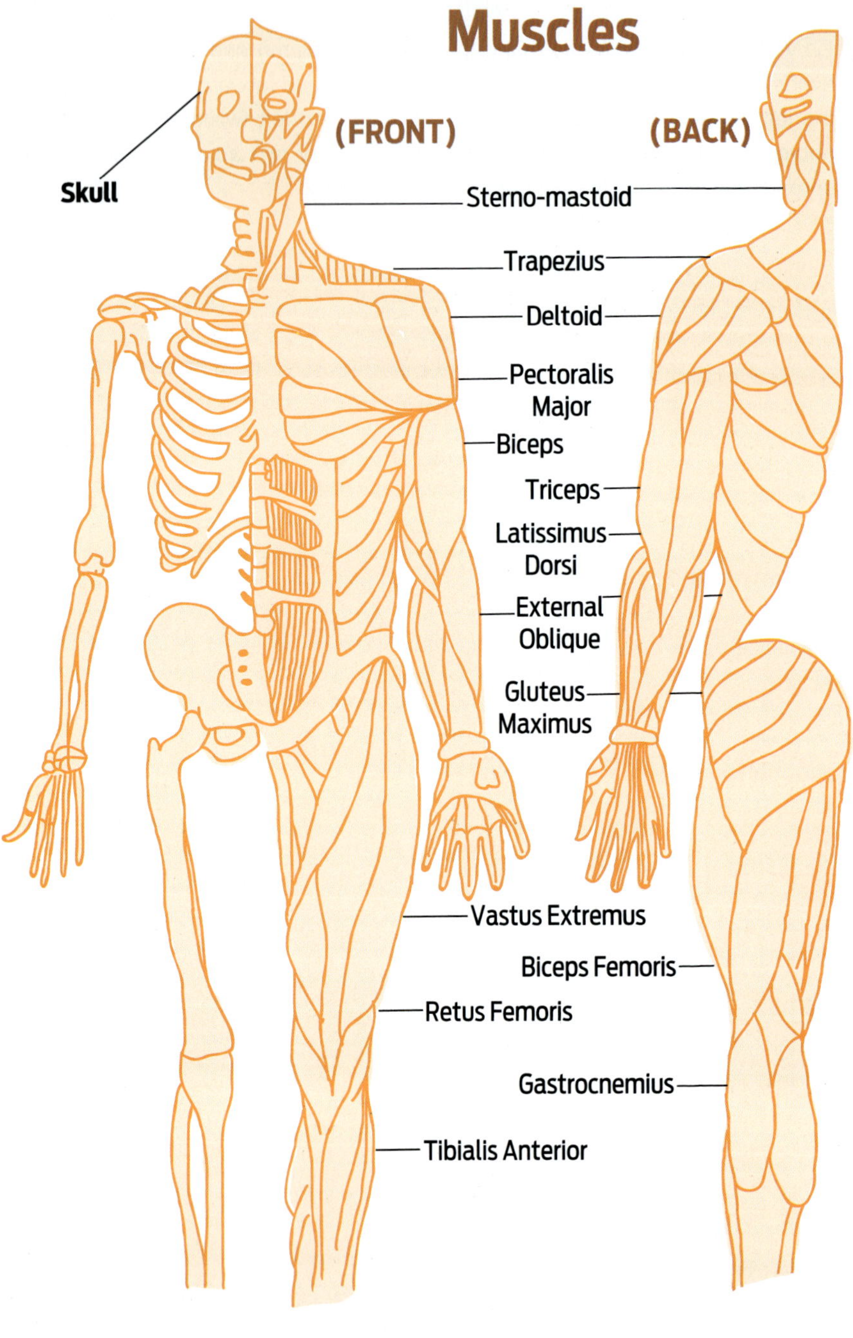
Muscles
(FRONT)
(BACK)
Skull
Sterno-mastoid
Trapezius
Deltoid
Pectoralis Major
Biceps
Triceps
Latissimus Dorsi
External Oblique
Gluteus Maximus
Vastus Extremus
Biceps Femoris
Retus Femoris
Gastrocnemius
Tibialis Anterior

FIG.3

The Muscular System

The muscular system consists of muscles about five hundred in number. They constitute what is popularly known as flesh. They not only cover the skeleton, but also occupy the deeper parts of the human body. The skeletal muscles are made up of small, elongated thread-like structures called muscular fibers. The muscular coats of the stomach, the intestines etc., are made up of cells. When a muscle is working these fibers and cells contract and consequently become shorter. The result is that the whole muscle is contracted and becomes shorter. When a muscle composed of fibers is at work, it not only becomes shorter but also thicker in the middle. This thickening of the muscle in the middle can best be felt and seen in the case of our biceps. This muscle crosses our upper arms in the front and its work is responsible for bending our forearms in the elbows. If we grasp our right arm with the left hand while the right elbow is straight and then if we bend the right forearm in the elbow, we find a muscle bulging out under our left hand. This muscle is the biceps and its bulging out is due to its thickening in the middle because of its activity.

All our physical movements are brought about by muscles that cover the skeleton. We can bring about any one of these movements at our will, simply because the muscles connected with these movements are under the control of our will. Hence, these muscles are called voluntary. There are other muscles, however, which we cannot contract at our will. Their work is being done independent of our will-power. Such muscles are called involuntary. The best examples of involuntary muscles are the stomach, the intestines and the heart. The walls of arteries are also made up of involuntary muscles.

We shall understand the working of the involuntary muscles when we come to the study of the different systems to which they belong. At present, we shall take into consideration a few voluntary muscles of importance.

The diaphragm is perhaps the most important voluntary muscle in the human body. Being strongly built it divides the thorax from the abdomen, serving as a partition between the two. The diaphragm is a dome-shaped muscle, the convex surface of it being turned towards the chest. It moves up and down several times a minute. When it descends the vertical capacity of the chest is increased, which leads to the act of inspiration. On the side of the abdomen this descent of the diaphragm exerts a gentle pressure upon the abdominal viscera and gives them a sort of massage, which helps considerably in maintaining their health.

The diaphragm is not, however, the only muscle that brings about respiration. There are other muscles which co-operate with the diaphragm in carrying on the respiratory function. These muscles are situated between the ribs and hence are called intercostal.

On the side of the belly there are a number of strong muscles which hold together the abdominal viscera. We might here take notice of only two of them, the two straight muscles that vertically cross the front of the abdomen. They are called abdominal recti. On the upper side they are attached to the ribs and on the lower side to the pubic bone. When they contract they give forward bend to the body. During respiration they move in co-operation with the diaphragm, and just like it massage the different organs held in the abdominal cavity and promote their health.

Having studied a few facts about the bones and muscles which form the bulk of the human body, we come to the nourishment of the cells of which the whole body is made.

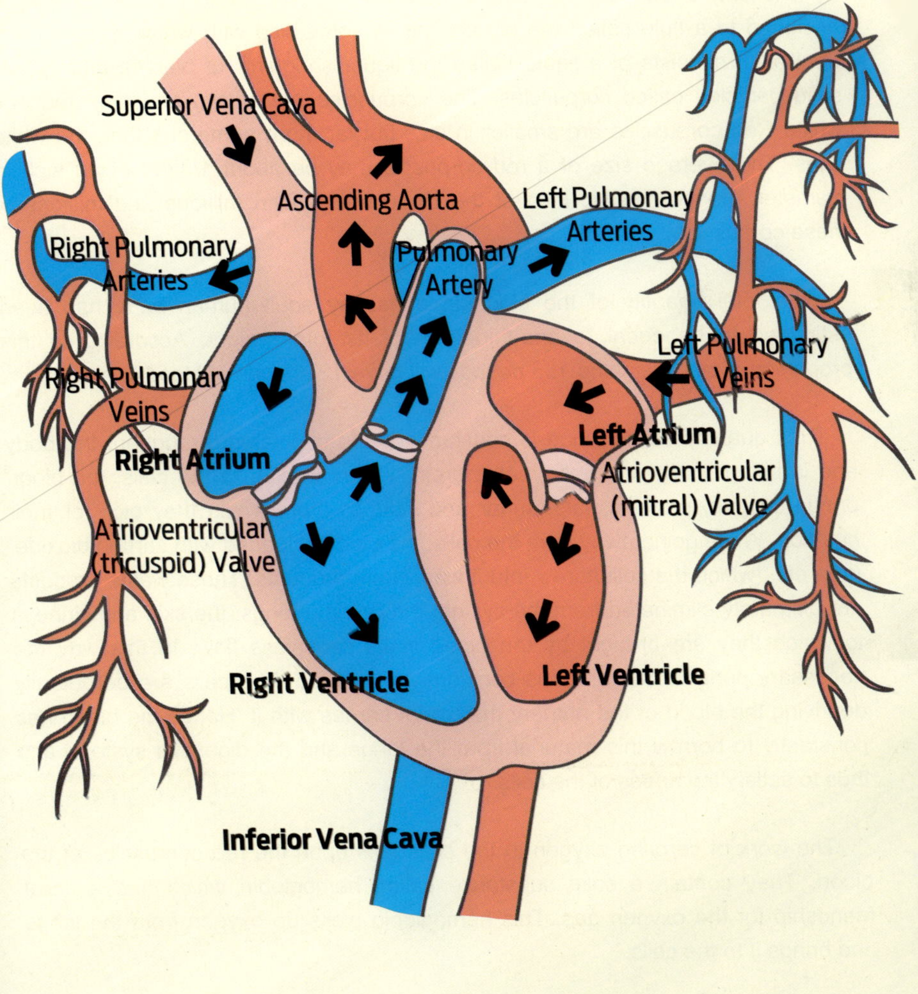
Superior Vena Cava
Ascending Aorta
Left Pulmonary
Arteries
Right Pulmonary
Arteries
Pulmonary
Artery
Left Pulmonary
Veins
Right Pulmonary
Veins
Left Atrium
Right Atrium
Atrioventricular
(mitral) Valve
Atrioventricular
(tricuspid) Valve
Right Ventricle
Left Ventricle
Inferior Vena Cava

FIG.4

The Circulatory System

The duty of carrying the nutrient material to every cell in the human body is assigned to a fluid called the blood. This is something with which every one of familiar. It consists of a liquid called the liquor sanguinis of plasma and minute solid particles called corpuscles. The corpuscles are of two varieties: red and white. Red corpuscles are smaller in size but far more numerous than the white ones. The average size of a red corpuscle may be about 1/3200 of an inch in diameter. Hence a cubic inch of the blood will contain millions and millions of these corpuscles.

The total quantity of the blood in a healthy adult human body has been estimated to be equal to one-thirteenth of its total weight. According to this proportion a man weighing 156 pounds will have 12 pounds of blood in him.

This quantity of the blood is constantly being circulated throughout the body and is being brought to every cell therein. When coming to the cells, the blood brings oxygen, proteins, fats, sugar and salts to them which they pick for their nutrition. While going away from the cells, the blood is loaded with carbon dioxide, urea etc., which the cells throw into it was waste products. These waste products are ultimately eliminated from the system through the lungs, the skin and kidneys to which they are brought by the blood in its ceaseless flow. In this way the necessary purity of the blood is constantly preserved. The cells are perpetually depriving the blood of the nutrient material it carries with it. Hence the blood has constantly to borrow this material from the lungs and the digestive system, and thus to satisfy the needs of the cells.

The work of carrying oxygen to the cells falls upon the red corpuscles of the blood. They contain a solid substance called hemoglobin which has a great friendship for the oxygen gas. This hemoglobin picks up oxygen from the lungs and brings it to the cells.

We have to note here the following characteristics of hemoglobin. When this substance combines with oxygen it becomes scarlet red in appearance, but when deprived of oxygen it becomes purple in colour. Further, if hemoglobin combines with carbon dioxide, its colour becomes entirely dark. These characteristics of hemoglobin will help us to understand the difference between the colour of the blood coming to the cells and the colour of the blood going away from them. Let us see how. When the blood is flowing to the cells, the hemoglobin in its red corpuscles is combined with oxygen, and has a bright red appearance which it lends to the whole quantity of the blood to which it belongs. But when the blood is flowing away from the cells, the hemoglobin of the red corpuscles becomes deprived of its oxygen. Not only that but it becomes combined with carbonic acid gas which the cells pass into the blood. Now the hemoglobin of the blood thus combined with carbon dioxide becomes dark in colour and lends a darkish appearance to the whole blood.

Up to now we have studied the nature of the blood and also the work it has to do in the human body. We shall now proceed to see what apparatus has been set up to keep the blood going on its ceaseless round.

This apparatus consists of the heart, the arteries, the capillaries and the veins. The heart is the central pumping station from which the fluid of the blood circulates in the body. A big tube starts from the heart which divides and subdivides itself several times till at last its branches reach every organ in the human body. This big tube is called the aorta and its branches leading to the different organs have their individual names, the aorta and its ramifications being called arteries. These arteries after reaching the respective organs become distributed into countless minute tubes the smallest of them having a diameter hardly bigger than 1/32000 of an inch. These hair-like tubes are called capillaries. These capillaries penetrate every organ so thoroughly that every cell of the organ is surrounded by them in every part of the human organism. This network of capillaries after penetrating every organ through and through, reunites to form bigger and bigger tubes, till at last two very big tubes are formed which completing the round of tubes open into the heart. The tubes which join the capillaries with the heart are called veins.

We shall now try to see something more of this apparatus which goes by the name of the circulatory system. The heart is a pear-shaped hollow organ whose walls are made up of an involuntary muscle. It is placed in the chest between the two lungs. (vide Fig. 5). The cavity of the heart is divided by a septum into two parts, the right and the left, the place of the septum being indicated by a groove which crosses the outer surface of the heart muscle. (vide Fig. 4). Again each of these two parts, the right and the left, is further divided into two chambers, ne upper and the lower. The upper chamber are called atria or auricles and the lower chambers are called ventricles. Thus there are four chambers - the right auricle, the right ventricle the left auricle, and the left ventricle. Between each auricle and ventricle there is a valve which allows the blood to pass from the auricle to the ventricle, but does not allow any blood to pass back from the ventricle to the auricle. Tubes in the form of arteries and veins stand connected with the heart.

We have already seen that the heart is an involuntary muscle. It contracts and relaxes something like 70 times a minute in a healthy individual. Its contraction is called systole while its relaxation is known as diastole. Systole is the time of action for the heart whereas diastole is the time of rest. It is to be noted that the heart does not contract as a whole at once, but the contraction takes place in parts, first in the two auricles and immediately thereafter in the two ventricles. Both auricles and ventricles relax after their respective periods of contraction when the whole heart is at rest. It is observed that diastole of the heart lasts a little longer than its systole. Hence they say that the heart sleeps for thirteen hours and works for eleven hours every day. The sleeping heart passively receives the blood from the body and the waking heart actively propels it into the body.

Let us now follow the current of the blood that is kept going round by the circulatory system. Two big veins, the superior vena cava and the inferior vena cava (vide Fig. 4). pour the blood into the right auricle of the heart. The superior vena cava drains those parts of the body that are situated above the level of the heart, whereas the other vein drains the remaining parts. While receiving this venous blood, the right auricle is in diastole. When full this auricle contracts and squeezes its contents into right ventricle which receives them passively, itself remaining in a relaxed condition. Now it is the turn of the right ventricle to contract and to force out the blood it contains into the pulmonary artery for being taken to the lungs. The blood received from the two caves is full of carbon dioxide which is to be eliminated. Hence the heart sends this blood to the lungs. There that gas is got rid of and fresh oxygen is picked up by the blood. When this is done the blood becomes charged with oxygen. It gets also its colour changed from purple to red scarlet. Now this oxygenated blood is to be distributed to the different cells in the body. For this purpose it is brought from the lungs to the heart by the pulmonary vein. The blood is first poured into the left auricle when the latter is in diastole. Thereafter that auricle contracts and forces the blood into the ventricle. The left ventricle then contracts and pushes out the blood into the aorta and its various branching arteries.

The left ventricle contracts with such a vigour that the blood forced out into the aorta is sent throughout its ramifications with a jerky motion. It is this jerk that constitutes the pulse which medical men feel in the patient's wrist. An idea of the vigour with which the left ventricle works can also be had by the feeling of the heart beat in the chest. This beat is the result of the left ventricle dashing itself against the chest wall while undergoing its forceful contraction.

During each contraction the heart propels about four ounces of the blood into the arteries. We have seen that the heart contracts 70 times in a minute. Thus we find that every minute the heart pushes into the arteries as much as 280 ounces of the blood or in other words as much quantity of it as is sufficient to fill half a tin of kerosine oil!

From the arteries the blood passes into the capillaries and from the capillaries into the veins. Ultimately the two cavae gather the blood from all the veins and pour it into the right auricle.

The blood pushed into the arteries feels the propelling force of the heart every time. This force is the strongest just near the heart, but it becomes weaker and weaker as the blood gets further away. In the capillaries the propelling force becomes so weak that the blood loses the jerky motion which it has in the arteries. Hence the blood flow in the capillaries is smooth. In the veins the propelling force continues to weaken increasingly till it is entirely lost when the blood returns near the heart. In fact the heart has to suck up the blood from the veins that unite with it.

As stated above the blood squeezed out of the heart flows through the blood-vessels, namely, the arteries, the capillaries and the veins.

The arteries and the veins are made up of the same types of tissues. In some parts the elastic tissue predominates, in others, the contractile. But the arteries are far stronger in their structure than the veins. Hence when empty, veins will collapse, whereas arteries will maintain their tubular form. Even the weakest veins, however, do not allow the blood flowing through them to exchange its content with anything outside their walls. It is only in the capillaries that this change takes place, because, the walls of the capillaries are extremely thin. Thus the blood while going through the capillaries of the lungs exchanges its carbon dioxide with the oxygen of the air in the air-cells, and while passing through the capillaries of the other part of the human body, it exchanges its nutrient material including oxygen with the waste products of the cells, these waste products consisting of the carbonic acid gas etc.

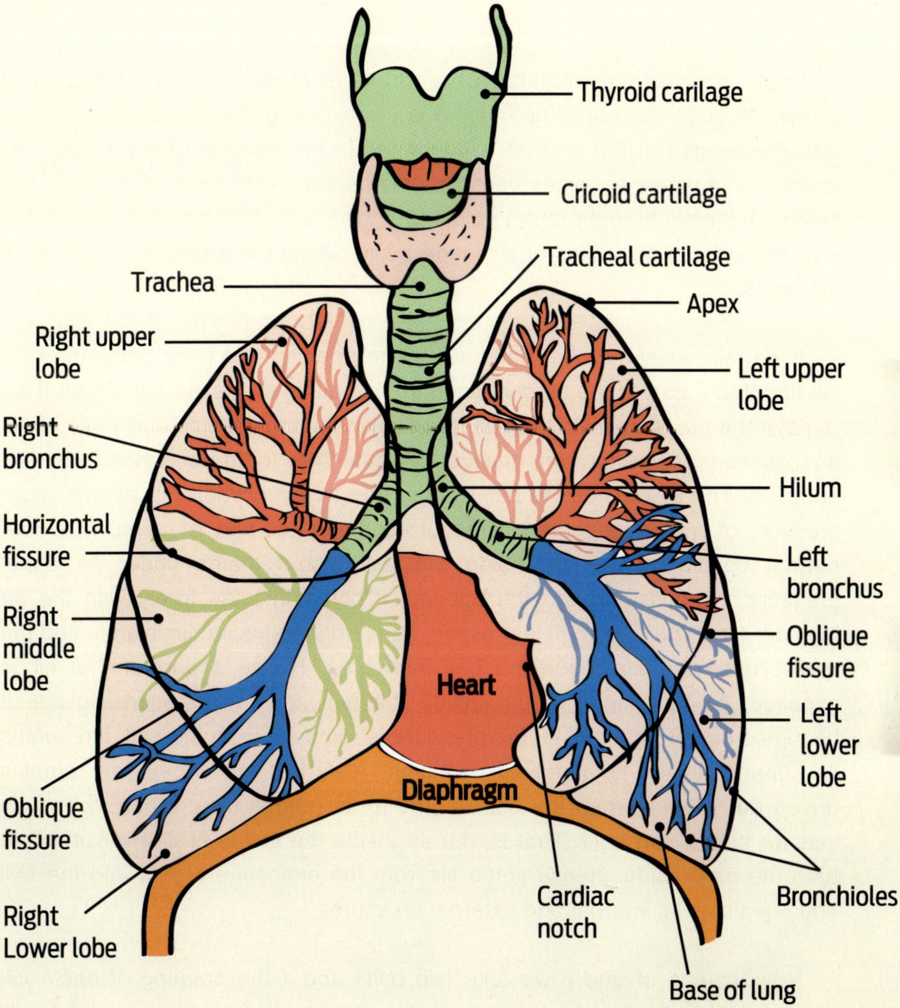
Thyroid carilage
Cricoid cartilage
Tracheal cartilage
Trachea
Apex
Right upper lobe
Left upper lobe
Right bronchus
Hilum
Horizontal fissure
Left bronchus
Right middle lobe
Oblique fissure
Heart
Left lower lobe
Diaphragm
Oblique fissure
Bronchioles
Cardiac notch
Right Lower lobe
Base of lung

FIG.5

The Respiratory System

In our study of the circulatory system we have seen that the blood when flowing through the capillaries of the lungs exchanges its carbonic acid gas with the oxygen of the air that is contained in the air-cells of the lungs. The exchange of gases becomes possible only because quantities of fresh air are being constantly brought to the pulmonary area. We shall now proceed to see how these fresh quantities of air made available for the gaseous exchange in the lungs.

If we take elastic rubber ball having one opening and if we press the ball, we find that a part of the air contained in the ball, is squeezed out. Again if we remove the pressure from the ball, it resumes its original size and while doing so it sucks up some air from outside. We shall now try to understand why this happens. The air outside the ball like the free air everywhere, is always under pressure of one atmosphere or pressure equal to 760 mm. of mercury.[1] Under normal conditions the air inside the ball also remains under an equal pressure, because through the opening it communicates freely with the air outside. Now when the ball is pressed, its internal capacity diminishes and the pressure on the air inside the ball increases. Hence a part of that air is expelled, so that the pressure inside the ball and the pressure outside it becomes equal. Again when the pressure is removed from the ball, it resumes its capacity in the compressed condition. A part of the original air remains driven out. Hence when the ball returns to its normal size, it has in it much less air than it can hold. That is, the air inside the ball is at a lower pressure than the air outside. Hence some air from the atmosphere gets into the ball and equalizes its internal and external pressures.

Now instead of one if we take two balls and if the opening of each ball were to end in a tube, the two tubes afterwards uniting into one, and if we fill up the balls with very elastic pieces of sponge through which air can penetrate, these balls will exactly illustrate the lungs. Let us see how.

---

1. This is the pressure of the atmosphere at the sea-level. As one rises higher up this pressure goes on decreasing proportionately.

There are two lungs, the right and the left. Both of them are made up of a spongy substance. This substance is divided into three parts in the right lung and into two parts in the left, each of the part being called a lobe. (vide Fig. 5). The spongy substance of each lung is held in an air-tight bag having coverings in close contacts with each other, so that the two coverings make one coat only. These coverings are called the pleurae.

The coat of each lung has only one opening. It is in the form of a tube called the bronchus. The tube connected with the left lung is known as the left bronchus whereas the tube connected with the right lung is known as the right bronchus. The two bronchi unite to form the trachea which opens into the throat, the throat in its turn communicating with the nose. It is through the bronchi, the trachea, the throat and the nose that the lungs keep communication with the outside atmosphere.

The two lungs are held in an air-tight cage called the chest. The sides of this cage are made up of the flexible ribs and its bottom is made up of a very stout muscle called the diaphragm. The ribs are moved up and down by means of the intercostals. Because of the action of the diaphragm and the intercostals, the chest expands and contracts, several times in a minute. Now when the chest contracts the lungs inside are pressed and the air contained in them is forced out, just as the air from the elastic rubber ball referred to in the last but one paragraph, is forced out under pressure. This going out of the air from the lungs is called exhalation. Again when the chest expands, the pressure in the lungs is lowered. Hence they suck up some air from the atmosphere. This sucking up of the external air into the lungs is called inhalation. Both inhalation and exhalation constitute the act of respiration and the apparatus used in this act is called the respiratory system.

In the foregoing paragraph we have seen how air is drawn into the lungs. We shall now see how it is brought close to the blood circulating through the lungs for an exchange of gases. We have referred to the bronchi which enable the lungs to communicate with the atmosphere. These bronchi after entering the lungs, divide and subdivide themselves into numerous smaller and still smaller tubular branches till their diameter measures hardly more than 1/40 of an inch. Here these fine bronchial tubes stop subdividing themselves further, but form very tiny air-cells roundabout them. When the air down into the lungs comes as far as these air-cells, it finds that the walls of the air cells are so thin that it can easily leak out if it is wanted outside the air-cells. Now forming a sort of network with the air-cells in the lungs are distributed the blood capillaries bringing from the heart quantities of the blood full of the carbonic acid gas. This gas the blood is anxious to get rid of and obtain oxygen instead for the nourishment of the cells all over the body. The walls of these capillaries also are so thin that they can allow carbon dioxide to escape and oxygen to come in its exchange. Even the combined thickness of the walls of the air-cells and capillaries is not sufficient to stop this exchange of gases. So the air from the lungs takes up carbon dioxide from the blood in the capillaries and lends instead its oxygen to the blood.

In every inhalation we take about 500 c. c. of air into the lungs. This contains a little less than 105 c. c. of oxygen. All this oxygen is not, however, taken up by the blood. The blood takes up only about 24 c.c. of it and returns in exchange nearly and equal quantity of the carbonic acid gas. So when the air comes out of the lungs, it contains all the carbonic acid gas taken from the blood and also a large quantity of oxygen that remains unabsorbed by the blood. The rate of respiration in a healthy adult is from 14 to 18 per minute.

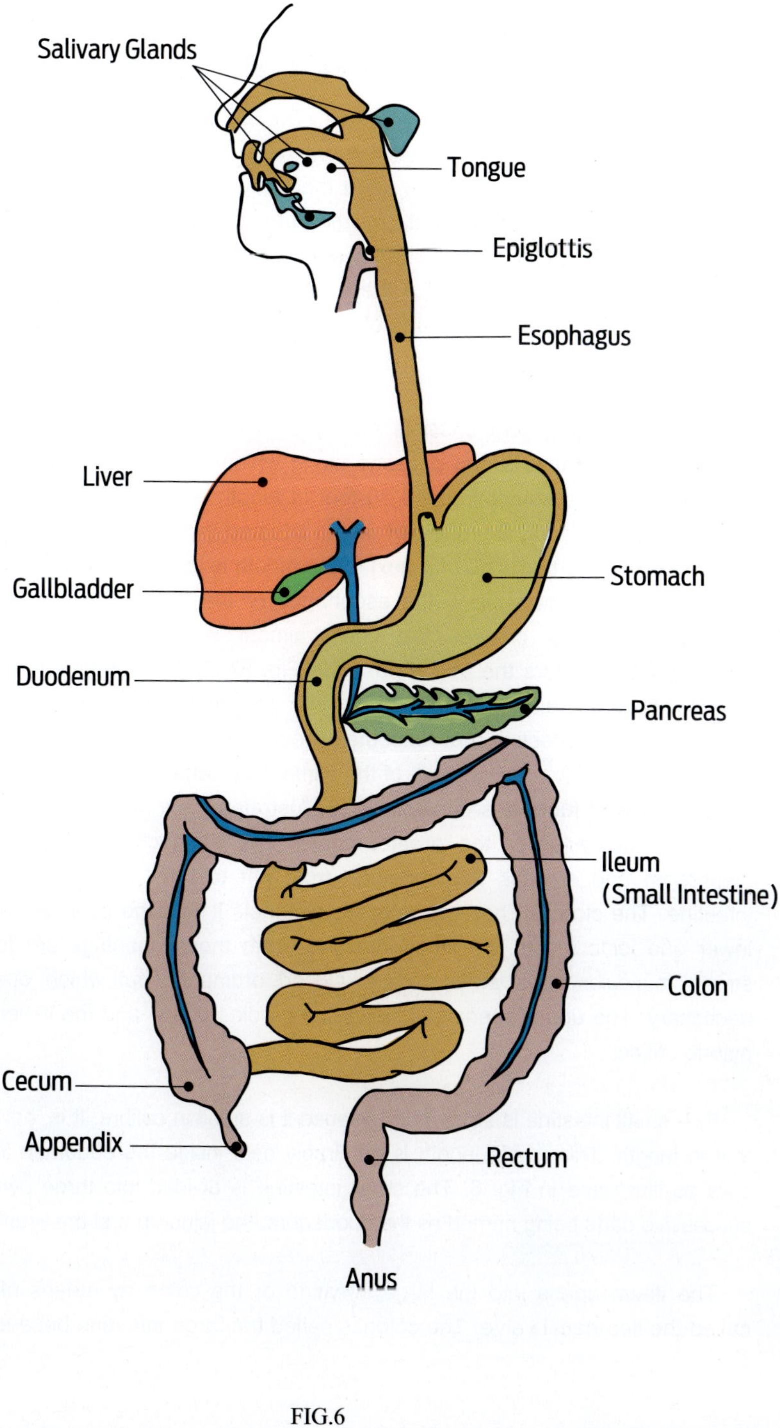

Salivary Glands
Tongue
Epiglottis
Esophagus
Liver
Stomach
Gallbladder
Duodenum
Pancreas
Ileum
(Small Intestine)
Colon
Cecum
Appendix
Rectum
Anus

FIG.6

The Digestive System

In our study of cells we have seen that they require oxygen, proteins, fats, sugars and salts for their life and growth. Out of these oxygen is supplied to the cells by the respiratory system. The system which is responsible for getting the other nutritive material ready for them is the digestive system. We shall now proceed to study the different parts of which this system is made up and the way in which it feeds the cells.

The digestive system consists mainly of a continuous tube known as the alimentary canal, that is, the passage along which the food passes through the body. This tube is something like 30 feet in length and starting from the mouth ends at the anus. Only a small part of it is situated in the chest, most of the tube being held in abdomen. The part next to the mouth is the pharynx which descends down the throat and ends in the esophagus or the gullet. Passing behind the trachea esophagus crosses the chest almost vertically, till it pierces the diaphragm and enters the abdomen. (vide Fig. 6). The esophagus is something like 9 inches in length. After coming into the abdomen in the form of the esophagus, the digestive tube becomes greatly dilated to form the stomach. So the stomach is only a dilated part of the alimentary canal. The stomach, however, is not a straight tube. It is curved. Fig. 6 illustrates the inner or the lesser curve and also the outer or the greater curve. The stomach lies just below the diaphragm and crosses the abdomen from left to right. It ends in the small intestine. The stomach has two opening connects it with the esophagus and the lower one joins it with the small intestine. Both these openings are formed of strong muscular rings which remain closed ordinarily, but which open when necessary. The upper opening is called the cardiac orifice and the lower one the pyloric orifice.

The small intestine is so named because it is small in calibre. It is, however, 22 feet in length. This whole length is admirably held inside the abdomen in several coils as illustrated in Fig. 6. The small intestine is divided into three parts, these successive parts being named as the duodenum, the jejunum and the ileum.

The ileum opens into the large intestine or the colon by means of a valve called the ileo-cecal valve. The colon is called the large intestine because of its big calibre which varies from 1.5 to 3 inches in diameter. The length of the colon is only 5 feet. In the abdomen it passes in a curve round the coils of the small intestine and gets different names for its different parts. The part of it which is below the ileo-cecal valve is called the cecum. To this cecum is attached externally a small organ called the appendix. This organ when inflamed gives rise to the disease appendicitis.

The colon ends in the rectum which is only some 6 inches in length. The last part of the colon, hence also of the digestive tube, is called the anal canal. It is only an inch in length. The rectum and the anal canal are continuous. The opening by which the digestive tube terminates is called the anus. It is guarded by a strong muscular ring which opens at the time of defecation, but otherwise remains contracted and closed.

The digestive tube is made up of strong muscular coats. A wave of contraction travels down the tube and pushes forth the food contents. Such a wave is called peristalsis. If the wave travels in the opposite direction, it takes the contents backwards. The backward wave is called anti-peristalsis. The action of vomiting is brought about by anti-peristalsis.

The inner surface of the whole of the digestive tube is lined with the mucous membrane, the same fine delicate thing that covers the cavity of mouth. Several glands are situated in this tube and pour their secretions into for helping digestive process. The salivary glands are located in the mouth, the gastric or peptic glands in the mucous membrane of the stomach and the intestinal glands in the mucous membrane lining the intestines.

No description of the digestive apparatus can be complete without taking into account two accessory glands, the liver and the pancreas.

The liver is the biggest gland in the human body. It weighs as much as 55 ounces. It is situated on the right side of the abdomen just below the diaphragm.(vide Fig.6). Its left part extends a little even beyond the breastbone. The liver plays a very important part in the digestive system. The venous blood carrying with it nourishing material collected from the stomach and the intestines has to pass through this gland and be worked upon by it. If the liver does not function satisfactorily this nourishing material suffers in quality and leads to various disorders. The liver is responsible for an important product called the bile. This product is generally first stored up in a vessel called the gall bladder (vide Fig.6), and then poured into the duodenum through the bile-duct.

The pancreas is much smaller than the liver. It weighs only 2 to 3 ounces and is irregularly prismoid in shape. It is situated behind the stomach. This gland has a secretion which is poured into the duodenum along with the bile and is known as the pancreatic juice. It plays a very important part in the digestion of food.

Thus far we have considered the digestive apparatus. Let us now see how this apparatus digests the food that we take and how it sends the nourishing material on the cells.

In order to understand the problems of digestion and nutrition, it is necessary for us to know a few chemical and physical facts. Chemically examined the different articles of food we take fall into four heads, namely, proteins, carbohydrates, fats and salts. Out of these carbohydrates contain starches and sugars. It is possible for the constituents of an article of food to fall under a single category, but generally foodstuff combines the different chemical varieties noted above. For instance sugar falls under carbohydrates only. Ghee is nothing but fat. But wheat bajari or rice is a combination of proteins, fats and carbohydrates; whereas milk contains all the four varieties mentioned above. Of course the proportion of different varieties differs in different foodstuff. For example, the percentage of fat present in rice is only 0.4, but in wheat it is 1.7 and in buffalo's milk 9. Another fact which needs our attention in regard to these chemical constituents of food is their solubility or otherwise in water. Salts and sugars are soluble in water whereas proteins, starches and fats are insoluble. Now the membrane which covers the inner surface of the digestive tube allows only those chemical substances to pass through it which are soluble in water. Hence salts and sugars can pass through the membrane, but proteins, fats and starches cannot. We have, however, seen that the cells of the human body constantly stand in need of not only salts and sugars, but also of proteins, fats and starches. Now these latter varieties of food constituents, if they are to reach the cells, must do so, by getting into the blood current, and they can get into the blood current only if they can pass through the membrane. Again they can pass through the membrane, only if they are rendered soluble in water. This is exactly what is done by the process of digestion. The different glandular secretions that are poured into the food tube, act upon the constituents of the food we take, and render them soluble in water. So we can define digestion as the process by which the different constituents of the foodstuffs are rendered soluble in water by the action of the glandular secretions of the alimentary canal, so that they could get into the current of the blood and be carried to the cells of the body for their nourishment.

Having studied the general nature of digestion, let us now know some details of this process. As seen in the last paragraph, out of the foodstuffs we take, sugars and salts are soluble in water and can pass to the blood current directly. But the starchy part of carbohydrates, so also proteins and fats require to be made soluble before they can pass through the mucous membrane of the food tube. Let us now see how this is accomplished.

The first operation which the food we take undergoes, is its mastication. It is necessary for the foodstuff to be very powdered even while it is still in the mouth. The different juices which bring about digestion can act upon the food far more thoroughly, if the foodstuff is reduced to minute particles. Hence the need of thoroughly chewing our food whenever it is taken. Further the process of digestion starts right from the mouth. Saliva which is liberated by the salivary glands acts upon the starchy part of carbohydrates of our food and converts it into sugar thus rendering it soluble in water. Saliva which ordinarily keeps the mouth moist, moistens the masticated food and also helps us in swallowing it comfortably. As our experience tells us dry stuff is so difficult to be pushed down the throat. After getting into the stomach through the gullet, the food comes into contact with the gastric juice which is secreted by the gastric or peptic glands situated in the mucous membrane of the stomach. This juice acts upon the proteins and turns them into the peptones which are soluble in water. From the stomach the food goes into the small intestine. Here it meets with the pancreatic juice which is a very powerful digestive agent. It acts on all the insoluble constituents of our food, namely, starches, proteins and fats. Out of these, fats are digested almost exclusively by the pancreatic juice. But in the cases of proteins and starches the work of the pancreatic juice is only supplementary. If a part of starches escapes the action of saliva or a part of proteins escapes the action of the gastric juice, these parts are taken care of by the pancreatic juice and the work of the saliva and the gastric juice is completed by it. It is to be remembered that the bile from the liver and the secretion of the intestinal glands also play some part in the process of digestion. While these different secretions are acting upon the food, it is travelling down the digestive tube; and by the time the food reaches the end of the small intestine, the process of digestion is almost completed.

Thus we see that the different constituents of our food are digested in the alimentary canal because of the action of different juices poured into it by various glands. These digested constituents having been rendered soluble in water become dissolved in it and a sort of solution is prepared. We have already seen that the membrane covering the inner surface of the digestive tube is so thin that it allows such a solution to pass through it. Now just beyond this membrane there is the blood current circulating through the capillaries. The walls of these capillaries too are very thin and allow the foodstuff to get right into the blood current. This passing of the digested food into the circulatory system for being carried to the cells all over the body, is known as absorption. Ultimately when the cells pick up the nutritive elements from the blood and utilize them for their nourishment, the process is known as assimilation or nutrition.

The process of digestion starts in the mouth, but the process of absorption begins in stomach. Whatever part is thoroughly digested becomes dissolved in water and is absorbed by the walls of the alimentary canal. Thus the stomach is responsible for the absorption of salts, sugars and peptones, whereas the small intestine absorbs not only these but also fat. Most of our nutrition is absorbed through these two parts of the food tube. Absorption does take place in colon also, but this part of the bowel mostly extracts watery portions from the contents that are presented to it by the small intestine.

Bowel contents move very slowly through the colon. Food completes its journey of about 25 feet and reaches the ileo-cecal valve in four hours and a half, but it takes more than six hours to move along the 5 feet of the colon. Owing to this slow progress of the bowel contents in colon, the watery portion gets ample time for being absorbed into the system and by the time these contents reach the last part of the large bowel, they become semi-solid. There they lie till they are evacuated in defecation.

The food tube is made up of involuntary muscles. Hence their contraction which expresses itself in the form of peristalsis or anti-peristalsis is not under the control of our will. Students of Yoga can bring at least a part of these involuntary muscles under their control. But that is only an exception and not the rule. What is it then that ordinarily starts peristalsis and thus propels the food along the tube? Generally it is the chemical stimulus of the food itself. The chemical contents of food as it is being digested stimulate the nerves that control the intestinal muscles and set up a wave of peristalsis. In this connection the part played by the bile[1] is very important. It greatly helps the bowel movement because of its chemical nature. Mechanical stimulus is also a factor to be taken into account in studying

1. The bile is also responsible for not allowing the contents of bowels to purify.

the intestinal action. It has been found that peristalsis becomes weak if a particular amount of internal or external pressure is not exerted on the food tube.

The few facts about the digestive system that we noted up to now, will show that digestion is bound to suffer if the juices necessary for this process are not available or being available are not of the necessary strength. This is exactly what happens in the case of the disease called dyspepsis. Again the peristaltic action of the food tube must be such as would push the contents right up to its end throw them out. If this action is either weak or absent, constipation is the result. Either in dyspepsia or in constipation, foodstuff delayed in the tube begins to putrefy and dangerous toxins are manufactured. The process of absorption that is ever going on, puts these toxins into circulation throughout the system and poisons the different organs of the body. Hence health can be ensured only if the digestive system is able not only to digest the food but also to excrete the undigested and undigestable foodstuff.

Along with the digestive secretions, the bowels throw into the tube other things which are to be eliminated. So the ordinary stool consists of not only the undigested and undigestable food residue, but also some other things which the system does not want.

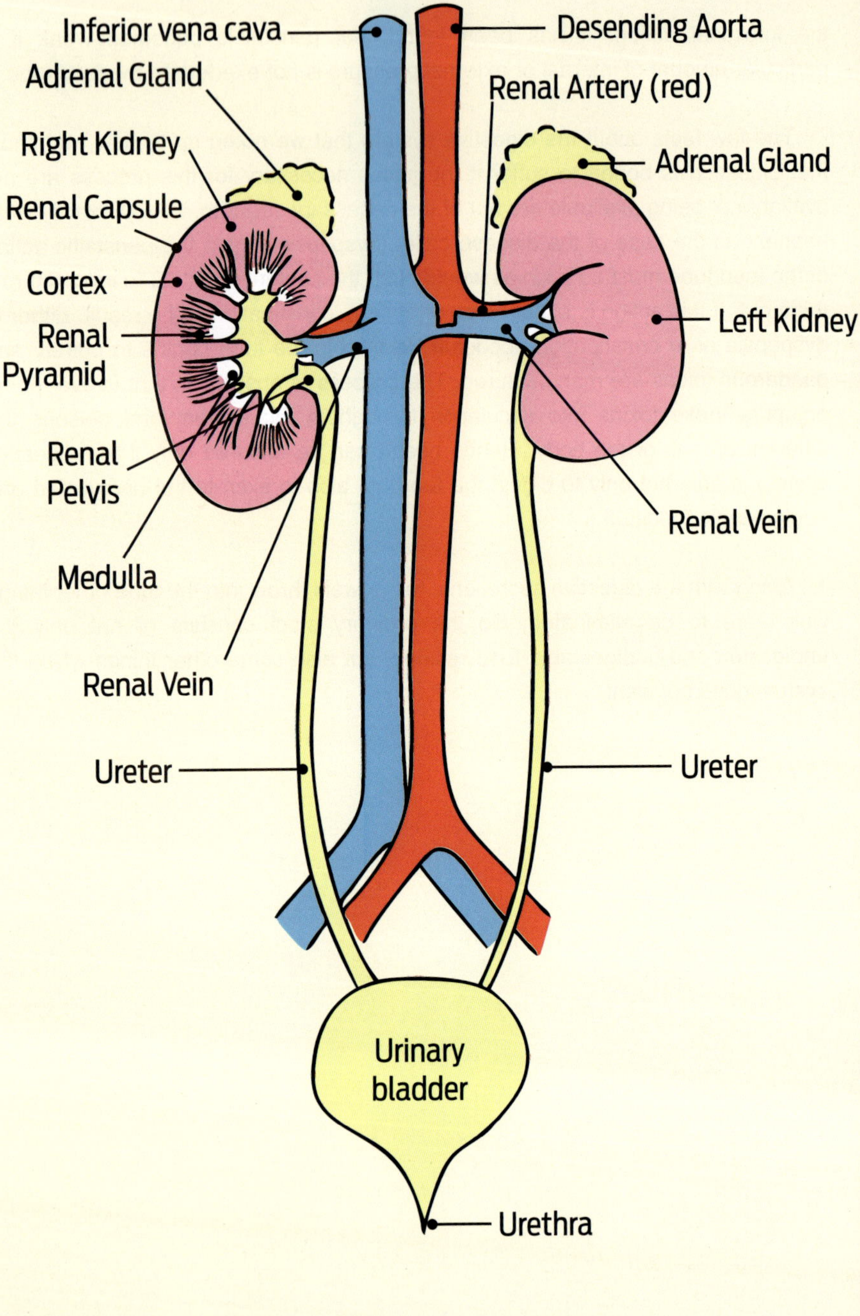
Inferior vena cava
Desending Aorta
Adrenal Gland
Renal Artery (red)
Right Kidney
Adrenal Gland
Renal Capsule
Cortex
Left Kidney
Renal
Pyramid
Renal
Pelvis
Renal Vein
Medulla
Renal Vein
Ureter
Ureter
Urinary
bladder
Urethra

FIG.7

The Urinary System

In the foregoing part of this chapter we have seen that the food tube acts not only as an organ of digestion but also as an organ of excretion. There are other organs which have an equally important excretory function. They are the kidneys. Connected with the kidneys are the ureters, the bladder and the urethra. All these organs constitute what is called the urinary system. While the body is functioning, it produces two important substances called the uric acid and urea. It is necessary for the human organism not to retain these substances beyond a particular measure, otherwise they lead to trouble. The work of duly driving out uric acid and urea is done by the kidneys. They excrete a fluid called the urine in which these substances are held in solution. The kidneys are situated in the back side of the abdomen. Each of them has a tube called the ureter passing from it to the bladder which is a muscular bag situated in the pelvis. Urine is secreted drop by drop and trickling down the ureters is collected in the bladder. When this bag is full we get a call for passing urine. If this is not suppressed the bladder contracts and expels urine through a passage which is called urethra. With urine both uric acid and urea are excreted. Failure of the urinary system to the function satisfactorily leads to the accumulation of the uric acid and urea in the system causing different disorders therein.

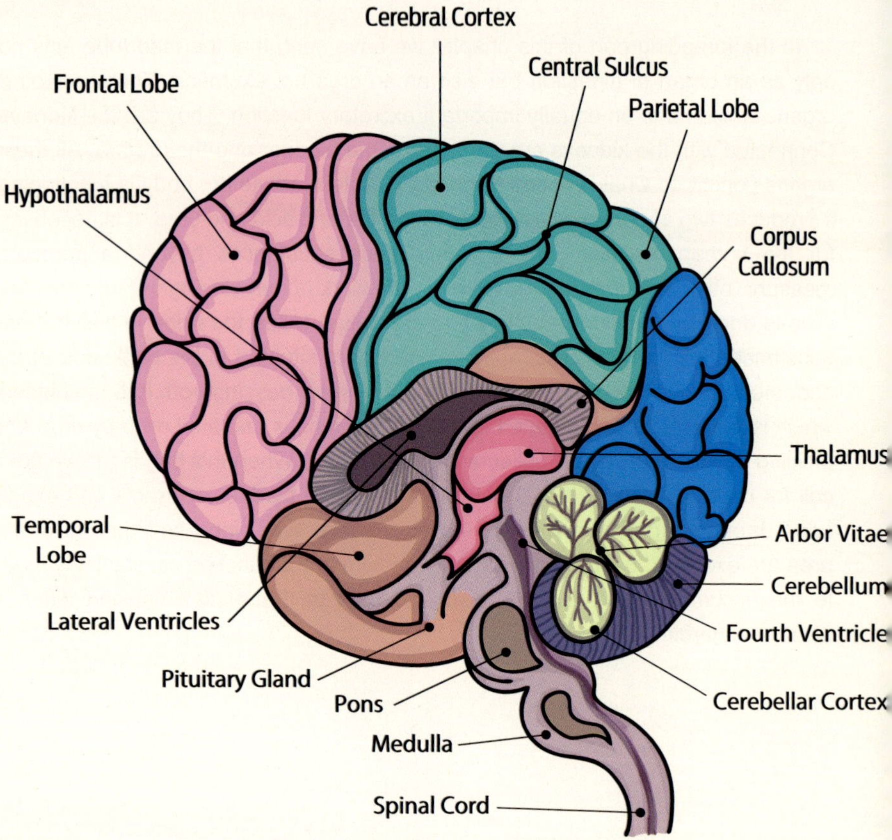
Cerebral Cortex
Central Sulcus
Frontal Lobe
Parietal Lobe
Hypothalamus
Corpus Callosum
Thalamus
Temporal Lobe
Arbor Vitae
Cerebellum
Lateral Ventricles
Fourth Ventricle
Pituitary Gland
Pons
Cerebellar Cortex
Medulla
Spinal Cord

FIG.8

The Nervous System

Up to now we have seen how nutrient material is introduced into the human body through the respiratory and the digestive systems and how the material thus introduced is taken to the different organs through the circulatory system. We have also seen how the excretory organs such as the lungs, the food tube and the kidneys throw out waste products. This study is sufficient to show that there is a sort of co-ordination amongst these systems working in the human organism. But if we observe things more closely this co-ordination becomes more evident. Let us watch a man, who is engaged in doing some violent muscular work. We find that his respiration becomes more and more rapid and that his heart begins to beat faster and louder. This shows that the work the man is doing with his muscular system affects his respiratory and circulatory systems also. Why is it so? It is because of the close co-operation of these three systems. Violent muscular work produces large quantities of carbon dioxide in the tissues. These abnormally large quantities must be brought to the lungs for being eliminated from the body and for this the heart must do additional work by making the blood circulation rapid. That is why the heart beats faster and louder. Again when the blood presents these extra large quantities of carbon dioxide to the lungs for elimination, the lungs must put in additional work for throwing them out through exhalation. Hence exhalation and consequently inhalation too become rapid.

But how is this co-operation brought about? Is there any agency which stands responsible for this co-operation? Yes, the system which brings about this co-operation is the nervous system. It is connected with all the different systems working in the human body where it controls their functions and co-ordinates them. In the instance of co-operation we referred to, in the last paragraph, the abnormal quantities of carbon dioxide, thrown into the blood by the vigorously working muscles, require a message to be sent to two centers in the nervous system, communicating to them the necessity of rapid blood circulation and rapid respiration. These centers in their turn issue orders to the organs of circulation and respiration which in response immediately begin to do work on a larger scale. In this way all co-ordination in the different systems is brought about by the nervous system, its supreme ruling power making such a thing possible. Let us now study this nervous system in some detail.

The nervous system consists of two divisions, the central or the cerebrospinal system and the autonomic system. The latter is again divided into two parts; the sympathetic and the parasympathetic. The central nervous system mainly consists of the brain, twelve pairs of the cranial nerves, the spinal cord and thirty-one pairs of the spinal nerves. The sympathetic is chiefly represented by two chains of ganglia paced one on each side of the spinal column. The parasympathetic is found near the brain and the sacrum.

Out of the different parts of the nervous system referred to above, the brain and the spinal cord and collections of nerve-cells. The brain, somewhat globular in form, is situated in the skull and its principal part is known as the cerebrum. The spinal cord which is elongated in shape is a prolongation of the brain and is held securely in the hollow of the spinal column. As the cerebrum and the spinal cord constitute the main portion of the central nervous system, it also goes by the name of the cerebrospinal system. Cranial nerves start from the brain and come out of the cranium. The spinal nerves start from the spinal cord and issue out from the spinal column. All these forty-three pairs of nerves spread themselves throughout the body and form a closely woven network. Nerves are made of fibres. They have an appearance of a thread. As they spread out they divide and subdivide themselves, till they reach all the inner and outer parts of the body in fine fibres called nerve-endings. The whole surface of the human body is so thickly covered with these nerve-endings that not a pinpoint could be placed thereon without touching some one of them. That is why we are able to detect the slightest touch even of a very pointed instrument anywhere in our body. Each nerve, at its origin, is connected with a group of nerve-cells which has a specialized function and which is known as a nerve-centre.

Functionally these nerves may be divided into two principal classes: motor or efferent and sensory afferent. Motor nerves are responsible for all the muscular activities of man. In their case the impulse starts at the centre and travels along the nerve to its further end where it sets up action in the muscle connected with it. For instance when I wish to pick up a book from the table, that wish starts impulses in the brain which travelling along the nerves excite the muscles of my hand to do work. The work of the sensory nerves is just of the opposite nature. They carry impulses to the centers from the further ends of the nerves. In the brain these impulses are interpreted into sensations. Nerves responsible for the sense of sight, smell taste, touch etc., are all of this class.

The sympathetic nervous system mainly consists of two rows of ganglia, that is, groups of nerve-cells, mutually connected by means of cords composed of nerve fibres. Thus there are two gangliated cords, and they are placed one on each side of the spinal column. Branches starting from these cords spread themselves to the different glands and viscera situated in the thorax and the abdomen.

Life processes which are ever going on in our body without the intervention of our will, are all under the influence of the sympathetic nervous system. The manufacture of the bile in the liver, the secretion of the pancreatic juice in the pancreas, the peristaltic and anti-peristaltic actions of the intestines, the beating of the heart, the movement of the lungs, all are carried on by this part of the nervous system. As the sympathetic as well as the parasympathetic systems work their way independent of our will, they are called autonomic.

The foregoing study of the nervous system clearly shows that all other systems working in the body are under the influence of this system. In fact the nervous system rules the whole human organism. If the nerve supply of the particular organ is cut off, the organ immediately ceases to work and will ultimately be entirely useless. If the nerve supply of the hand is cut off, that hand will be immediately paralyzed in spite of its possessing well developed muscles. If the visual centre in the brain goes out of order, the man will not be able to see even when his eye is intact. Therefore, if all the bodily functions are to be satisfactorily carried on, the nervous system must be kept in a very efficient condition.

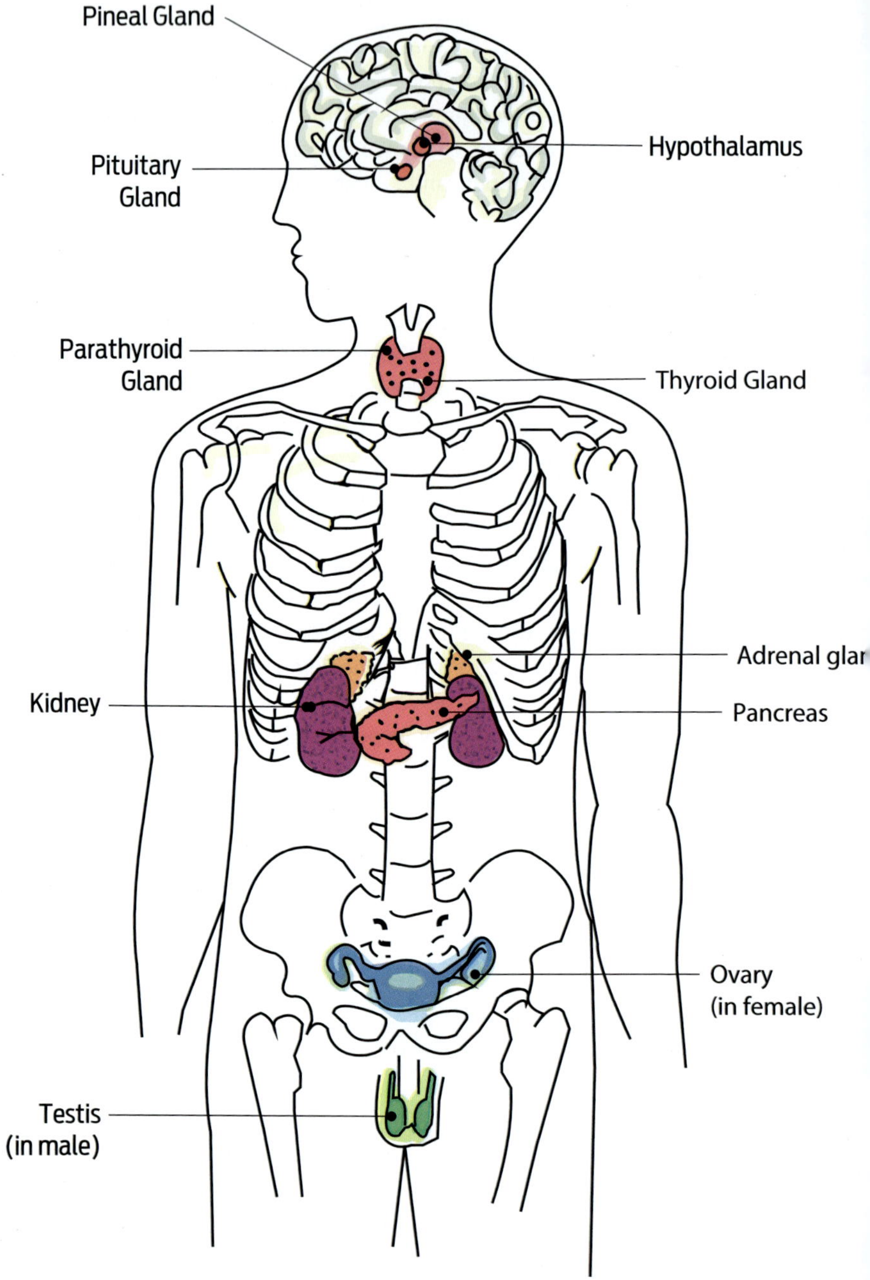
Pineal Gland
Hypothalamus
Pituitary Gland
Parathyroid Gland
Thyroid Gland
Adrenal glar
Kidney
Pancreas
Ovary (in female)
Testis (in male)

FIG.9

The Endocrine Glands

We cannot close this brief description of the human body without taking into consideration particular structures which influence all other structures in the human body including the nerves. These structures are known as the endocrine or ductless glands. These glands are called endocrine because they have an internal secretion as opposed to the external secretion like the bile of the liver or the pancreatic juice of the pancreas. External secretion leave the secreting glands through ducts such as the bile-duct or the pancreatic duct. But internal secretions are thrown directly into the blood current without their leaving the glands of the origin. Hence the endocrine glands have no ducts and that is why they are also called ductless. The endocrine glands are situated in the different parts of the body. Thus the thyroid and the parathyroid are situated in the neck. The pineal and the pituitary are situated respectively in the brain and at the base of the brain. The adrenals or the suprarenal glands are situated above the kidneys. The ovaries in the case of females are situated in the pelvis whereas the testes, the corresponding male reproductive structures, are held hanging in the scrotum.

In the human body there are some glandular structures which have both an internal as well as an external secretion. The best examples of these are the pancreas and the testes. The pancreatic juice which we have already studied is the external secretion of the pancreas. The external secretion of the testes is known as semen. From its origin it is conducted through ducts to two sacks situated in the pelvis and is stored up there before being utilized.

It has been experimentally found that the endocrine secretions very powerfully affect the nervous system, and through it, as well as otherwise, maintain the physiological balance of the human organisms. If these secretions suffer in quality pathological conditions in the different parts of the human body are rapidly established. We take a striking illustration of extreme pathological conditions arising from the withdrawal of the internal secretory activity of an endocrine organ. The menopause which is characterized by physiological cessation of menstruation, occurs when the ovaries cease to give their internal secretion. This leads to irritation or depression, vertigo, faintness, tachycardia, cold sensations in the hands and feet, vicarious bleeding from various parts of the body, and many other symptoms, which show that the whole bodily balance is upset.

Generally speaking the disturbances are not so universal, but are confined to particular parts of the body. Still these disturbances can amply prove the supreme importance of the internal secretion of the ovaries. The thyroid secretion provides another example. As soon as this secretion suffers, the cells of the most distant parts of the human body slowly begins to undergo a change. The hair begins to grow grey, the nails have a tendency to be brittle, fatty degeneration starts in the arteries, the face tends to be wrinkled, weakness creeps over the brain, in fact, many senile symptoms begin to be apparent.

Preparations containing internal secretions are made of the endocrine organs of animals and are used in the treatment of diseases. This is what constitutes organotherapy.

Yogic Therapeutics aims at restoring the internal secretions to their normality by securing the health of the endocrine organs through Yogic practices.

Conclusion

From the study of the different systems working in the human body, it is clear that their aim is to bring nutrition to the millions of cells of which the body is composed and to repair the constant waste which these cells undergo because of their ceaseless activity. This process is called anabolism. These two processes put together are known as metabolism. When anabolism is more active than catabolism the body gets an opportunity to grow. But when catabolism is more rapid than anabolism the body loses. In a growing child the anabolic process more than makes up the waste brought about by catabolism. Hence in the case of such a child there is constant development of the body. In a healthy adult both the anabolic and catabolic processes balance themselves and thus enable him to keep up his body unimpaired. In old age catabolism gets the upper hand and leads to a steady wastage of tissues.

In our study of this chapter we have seen that the different physiological systems of the human body are mutually co-operating with one another. When this co-operation is perfect, harmonious physiological functioning is ensured. This harmony is known in the ordinary language as health. If any of the system fails to co-operate, his harmony is disturbed and disease sets in. The aim of Yoga on its physical side, is to avoid disease and ensure health by establishing and maintaining physiological harmony in the human body.

2

PREPARING ONESELF for ĀSANAS

Yoga has a complete message for humanity. It has a message for the human mind. And it has also a message for the human soul.

Yoga-Śāstra unmistakably recognizes the interdependence of body and mind. It prescribes exercises both for the body and mind, so that the two might develop themselves in a spirit of co-operation to such a balanced psycho-physiological condition that they should cease to enslave the human soul. Yogins are convinced that thus freed from the thralldom of body and mind, the soul realizes its boundless existence of infinite bliss.

While acknowledging the interdependence of body and mind, Yoga Shastra holds that the influence of the mind on the body is far more powerful than the influence of the body on the mind. Hence mental exercises from the bulk of the Yogic curriculum, although physical exercises have also a definite place in it. Āsanas are physical exercises. They form the third item of the Yogic curriculum.

Yamas[1] and Niyamas[2] are mental exercises. They form the first two items. Yamas and Niyamas are given precedence in the curriculum, because without their practice, Āsanas will not give the desired results completely.

The preceding paragraphs have been written with a view to present to our readers the practice of Yamas, Niyamas and Āsanas in the right perspective from the point of view of Yoga-Śāstra. Out of the many points touched in these paragraphs, we shall now discuss at some length only those that directly concern a practical student of Yogic poses.

We shall start by making a brief reference to the results a student of Yoga expects to obtain from the practice of Āsanas. Next we shall examine the scientific evidence that is adduced to prove the interdependence of body and mind. Then we shall try to understand the general features of Yamas and Niyamas. When all this is done, we shall be in a position to see whether the practice of Yamas and Niyamas would enhance the results expected of Āsanas and whether the neglect of Yamas and Niyamas would impair the efficacy of these Yogic poses.

As will be clear from the following chapters, Āsanas are divided into two principal groups: Cultural and Meditative. Śīrsha, Sarvāñga, Bhujañga, Dhanus, Śalabha etc., are cultural whereas Padma, Siddha, Svastika and Sama are meditative. Individuals who take to the practice of Āsanas are also of two types: Those who seek only physiological advantages and those who are anxious to secure spiritual advantages also. People of the first type may be called physical culturists. In trying to obtain physiological results by the practice of the cultural poses, both spiritual culturists as well as physical culturists wish to maintain the nervous and endocrine system in excellent health, because through these two systems the health of the whole human organism can be secured, as we have seen in the first chapter of this handbook. A student of spiritual culture, moreover, undertakes to practice the cultural poses with an additional objects in view. He wants the nervous system to be so trained as would easily bear the interaction of the spiritual force called Kuṇḍalinī to awaken which is one of his principal aims.

---

1. अहिंसासत्याऽस्तेयब्रह्मचर्यापरिग्रहा यमाः । P.Y.S. II 30
(Inoffensiveness, truthfulness, non-stealing, continence, and non-receiving are the Yamas.)

2. शौचसन्तोषतपः स्वाध्यायेष्वरप्रण्धानानि नियमाहः । P.Y.S. II 32
(Purification, contentment, mortification, study and complete self surrender to the Lord are the Niyamas.)

Moreover, a student of spiritual culture would not be satisfied only with the cultural poses. He would very earnestly practice the meditative poses as well, because these poses reduce the metabolic activity of his body to a minimum and thus get the mind freed from all physical disturbances, so that it can be left to itself and be brought to a point, making concentration required for Dhāraṇā, Dhyāna and Samādhi possible. To put the whole thing in a nutshell, we can say that the cultural poses are practiced for training the nervous and endocrine system whereas the meditative poses are undertaken to eliminate physiological disturbances from the mental activity.

Having known the results Āsanas are expected to yield, we proceed to study the interdependence of body and mind. The old adage, sound mind in a sound body, unmistakably teaches the influence the body has upon the mind. The general experience that strong and healthy persons are of quite temperament whereas weak and unhealthy persons are irritable in temper, goes to prove that the body profoundly influences the mind. Take the case of a patient lying on his sick bed. He can rarely maintain his optimism when his health is rapidly ebbing. The same person begins to have a brighter outlook on life, the moment he begins to recover. It is well known that the drink habit can often be traced to the power of alcohol to free the individual from worries, never mind temporarily. The powerful influence the nervous system has upon the mind can easily be proved by taking into consideration the experience of constipated people. When their rectum is loaded with hard masses of fecal matter, the nervous system is very badly affected and this leads to terrible depression and very miserable brain fag. If in this condition, these persons clear their rectum by the use of the enema, they at once experience a spirit of exhilaration and their thinking becomes as clear as ever. The endocrine glands also have been found to influence the mind powerfully. In fact the most enthusiastic section of endocrinologists thinks that they can change the very temperament of individuals by treating their endocrine glands. All these facts go conclusively to prove that the body can powerfully influence the mind.

The influence of the mind on the body can also be proved on the strength of an equally convincing evidence. The aspect of mind which most powerfully affects the body and especially the nervous and endocrine systems is its emotional side. In order to understand how we are night and day under the influence of emotions, mild or violent, we have simply to know what emotions are and how they enter into our very being.

Love, anger, greed, infatuation, elation, hatred, jealousy, envy, fear, disgust, distress, regret, remorse, despondency, despair, confidence, hope, shame, pity, admiration, reverence, devotion, gratitude are all emotions.[1] Emotions of high intensity that last only for a short time are called passions. Thus the emotion of anger when it becomes violent the affected person flies into the passion of rage. The emotion of disgust when intensified develops into the passion of horror. Most of us have moods. They are emotions and differ from passions because of their longer duration and smaller intensity. When a mood becomes so habitual that it becomes a characteristic of an individual, it is called temperament. Now, although a few of us may be free from passions, every one of us has his own temperament and moods. Thus none of us is entirely free from emotions, Our very being is in the grip of our mind!

These emotions are found to affect our body more or less profoundly according to the degree of their intensity. Thus if the emotions are violent and sudden they may prove even deadly. The famous surgeon Vesalius dropped dead when he discovered that the dead body he was dissecting was still throbbing with life-blood in the heart. He was so powerfully overcome by sorrow. Even pleasing emotions may result in death. The deaths of the Greek tragedian Sophocles and the niece of Leibnitz are cases in points. One of the tragedies of Sophocles was awarded the highest prize. This so much filled him with joy that the emotion proved fatal. The niece of Leibnitz discovered a large amount of gold under the bed of her dead uncle. A terrible emotion of joy seized her and put an end to her life. If the effect of joy is identical with that of sorrow, it is because in both these cases what really takes effect is the surprise, the overwhelming astonishment which is common to both.

When the emotions are not so powerful, but are less violent, they may not lead to death, but they may so affect the nervous system that some disease may appear as a consequence. Prof. Naunyn states that after the bombardment of Strasburg in the year 1870, many cases of diabetes developed in consequence of the fear and anxiety brought about by it.

---

1. It will be readily seen that the first six emotions respectively represent काम, क्रोध, लोभ, मोह, मद, और मत्सर which are said to be the foes of the higher interests of man. After studying the present chapter our readers will see that they are the enemies of our physical health also.
The Bhāgavadgītā mentions the first three as destructive forces working against the spiritual growth of an individual as they try to drag him to hell.
Cf. त्रिविधं नरकस्येदं द्वारं नाशनमात्मनः
काम: क्रोधस्तथा लोभस्तस्मादेतत्त्रयं त्यजेत् ।। B.G.XV-21

These disturbances of the nervous system lead to the degeneration of the ductless glands which are admittedly governed by the sympathetic and the vagus. Doctors Lorand, Sajous and many others have conclusively proved that the soundness of different vegetative functions depends mainly on these ductless glands; and that if their internal secretions suffer, premature old age and even premature death may follow. Thus emotions, by causing the degeneration of the nervous system and also of the ductless glands, prove to be a serious disturbance to the health of the human body.

As we already know from the first chapter of this handbook, the most important ductless glands in the body are the thyroid, pituitary, adrenals and gonads or the sexual glands. We shall see how these several glands are affected by emotions.

The effect of emotions on the adrenals is to produce higher blood pressure which favours the development of arteriosclerosis and other diseases of the circulatory system.

The thyroid is so much affected by mental depression that this emotion is mentioned by scientists as one of the causes of myxoedema. This gland is one of the most powerful agencies set up by nature to protect the body against poisons. A degenerated thyroids means disease and even premature old age. So serious is the effect of continued mental depression upon the human body.

The pituitary is also affected by emotions. Prof. Pel and others have noted cases of acromegaly after violent emotions. Dr. Sajous has often pointed out this gland as the central organ upon which all strong emotions react.

Sexual glands are also powerfully influenced by emotions. Cases are often noted where menstruation has suddenly appeared after violent mental shocks. In the case of males emotions at times result in impotence.

In the previous paragraph we have referred to the effects of violent emotions upon the human body. Emotions that are less violent, although they do not immediately show any serious disturbances, surely have an injurious effect upon the different systems of the human organism.

Up to now only the adverse effects of emotions have been discussed. This should not mean that all emotions are injurious. There are particular emotions which exercise a healthy influence upon the nervous system. Hope and confidence which invariably enable a man to maintain an optimistic frame of mind always promote the health of the nerves. Joy and happiness kept within proper limits are of great help in building a healthy nervous system. Devotion to the Lord or in fact to any principle of life that ensures mental peace enables a person to maintain healthy and stable nerves.

We believe the evidence that we have put forth up to now is sufficient to establish the interdependence of body and mind. Both of them affect each other favourably as well as adversely. But if we probe the question of this interdependence a little deeper, we find that the mind has the strength to rise superior to all the influences of the body. To verify the truth of this statement we have simply to study the lives of the heroes of different nations who had to undergo terrible physical sufferings in order to serve their motherland. Their iron will not only knew no bending but it ever grew stronger and stronger as they were forced to face physical tortures. We read the glorious history of religious martyrs who did not in the least swerve from their convictions even when their bodies were actually burnt to ashes!

On the contrary we find the strongest bodies being paralyzed, if the man is overcome by fear. The healthiest constitutions are shattered under the baneful influence of worries. Physical giants actually totter when in a fit of rage and are not able to effectively use their strength. We personally know two youths turned impotent in a moment because of an imaginary misgiving!

This should convince us beyond any shadow of doubt that even when there is interdependence between body and mind, the influence of the mind on the body is far more profound than the influence of the body on the mind.

Reverting to our practice of Yogic poses, as we shall see from the subsequent chapters, these poses are bodily practices calculated to bring about particular physiological results. Now knowing as we do the profound influence of the mind on the body, can we think of training our body without undertaking the training of our mind! Can we ever hope to build a healthy thyroid or powerful sexual glands by means of Sarvāṅgāsana, if we allow our mind to run riot in the body and permit ourselves to be visited by terrific sexual storms shattering the tissue of the endocrine structures? Can Śīrṣāsana ever give us mental peace and vigour, if we suffer the canker of worries to eat into the very cells of our brain? We are sure our readers will answer these questions emphatically in the negative, because we believe that they stand convinced by now that physical training will never give the desired results unless and until it is backed up by mental training. So the two trainings must go hand in hand or to put the matter more accurately, mental training should be given precedence over physical training.

This is exactly why Yoga-Śāstra has placed Yamas and Niyamas as the first and second items of Yogic curriculum and has assigned Āsanas the third place. Yamas and Niyamas put together constitute ten principles of conduct which, if followed faithfully, invariably give supreme mental peace to a student of Yoga. He is freed from all violent emotions. His adamantine faith in the Lord develops in him a robust optimism. He maintains a clear conscience and can carry the sunshine of happiness wherever he goes. In short, he is able to ensure perfect health for his mind.

It is frankly admitted that perfection in the practice of Yamas and Niyamas is extremely difficult of attainment. Not even one in a million can make even a near approach to this perfection. But the incalculable value of Yamas and Niyamas lies in their capacity to bestow mental health even on those who sincerely try to make a humble beginning. Of course the degree of health will vary according to the degree of sincerity and the measure of success achieved. But even the meanest success will never fail to bring its heavenly blessings to the aspiring individual. So what is required as a preparation for Āsanas is only a determined effort to practice Yamas and Niyamas with a view to develop a healthy mind.

We do not want our readers to carry the impression that the practice of Āsanas cannot be started unless and until one achieves a certain degree of success in the observance of Yamas and Niyamas. In fact, the two practices may start at one and the same time. What we want to impress upon our readers is the necessity of putting into, practice Yamas and Niyamas, if Āsana are to be made to yield the best results.

Here some of our readers who look to Yoga from the point of view of physical culture only, may put forth the following argument. If the rigorous mental hygiene of Yamas and Niyamas is absolutely necessary for a successful practice of Āsanas even as forming a system of physical culture, these Āsanas stand at a tremendous disadvantage when compared with other systems of physical culture which do not require any mental discipline. Such an argument is unsound for

the following reasons.
(1) It has already been pointed out that the only thing required of a student of Āsana is a determined attempt to practice Yamas and Niyamas. None should be alarmed at the names of Yamas and Niyamas. Expressed in the ordinary language their practice on a humble scale means nothing more than moderation in every habit of ours with aliving faith[1] in our Maker.
(2) Unluckily it is a fact that the advocates of other systems of physical culture do not insist upon mental culture to proceed along with the physical training. But this does not mean that these systems can ensure physical health in spite of mental disadvantages. The interdependence of body and mind is a scientific fact common to all individuals whether they practice Yogic or some other system of physical culture. We are sure that the result of other systems would be far more encouraging if they also required their followers to practice mental hygiene simultaneously with the physical exercises.

Thus we see that the observance of Yamas and Niyamas is the most essential preparation for the practice of Āsanas.

Some rules have been laid down for the students of Āsanas in Appendix 1 in this handbook. They represent the irreducible minimum of Yamas and Niyamas.

Appendix 1 also states some of the minor requirements of people preparing themselves for the practice of Āsanas.

Now we shall close this chapter with a few words of advice to the students of meditative poses.

Meditative poses are of the highest value to a student of spiritual culture. They establish in the body such physiological conditions that the mind ceases to be disturbed by any stimuli received from the body. In fact the body stops entering into consciousness altogether. All this becomes possible only after a continued practice of one of these poses for a period of at least six months. One or even two hours must be devotedly given to some one of the meditative poses almost without a break. If this is done, appreciable results will follow in six months and the mind will be left to itself without any interference from the body.

---

1. This should not interpreted to mean that atheists cannot take to the practice of Yogic poses. We, however, certainly want to say that all other things being equal, a genuine theist can practice Āsanas with greater advantage than an atheist.

It must be, however, borne in mind that all this physiological advantage will not help a spiritual culturist in a substantial degree in concentrating his mind, if he does not scrupulously and zealously take to the observance of Yamas and Niyamas. Meditative poses will, indeed, free the mind from physical disturbances, but its wandering propensities will never stop and it can never be brought to a point unless it becomes free from emotions mild or intense. So in the case of spiritual culturists, the practice of Yamas and Niyamas on the largest possible scale is an absolute necessity. This is the one preparation without which it is impossible for him to make any headway in concentration.

We shall now refer to two minor preparations for the meditative poses and finish. A student of meditative poses should fix up for his work a place from which he can exclude all disturbing factors. In his case the need for utmost concentration is extreme. Hence it is desirable that he chooses a thoroughly ventilated room which is free from mosquitoes etc., and where he would be left to himself. Even the possibility of being disturbed by somebody comes in the way of perfect concentration. If he could reserve a room for this work and build up a spiritual atmosphere there, it will help him a good deal in his work.

So far as his seat is concerned, the traditional arrangement of seating is excellent. A carpet of Kuśa[1] grass, with a well tanned deer-hide[2] spread on it, the hide in its being covered with a daily washed piece of thick khaddar, makes a very comfortable seat. The pleasures of such a seat are the peculiar privilege of those God-intoxicated aspiring souls who seek salvation through Yoga. The thrilling spiritual experiences that this seat affords to the student from day to day, make it more attractive to him than even the throne of an emperor!

---

1. In the absence of Kuśa carpet, any other grass will do.

2. Those that may have a conscientious objection to the use of a hide should make use of a thick woolen cloth folded over several times.

3

MEDITATIVE POSES

Nāsāgra-Dṛṣṭi
Bhrūmadhya-Dṛṣṭi
Uḍḍiyāna-Bandha
Jālandhara-Bandha
Mūla-Bandha
Padmāsana
Siddhāsana
Svastikāsana
Samāsana

Note—Two Dṛṣṭi and three Bandhas are a part of the technique of the meditative poses. We begin this chapter with a description of these Dṛṣṭi and Bandhas, with a view to enable our readers to follow the technique of the Āsanas without any interruption.

Nāsāgra-Dṛṣṭi or The Nasal Gaze

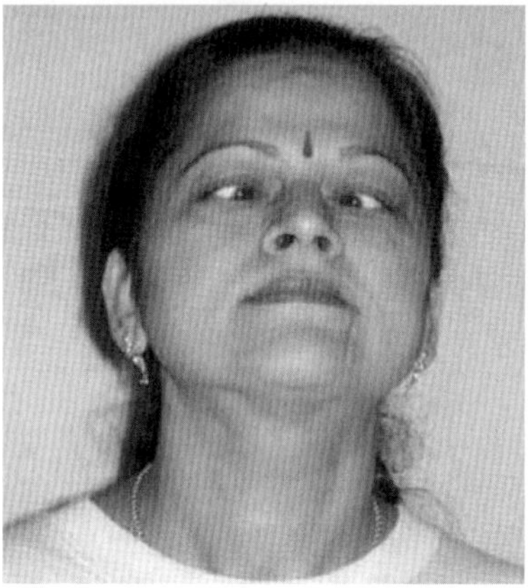

FIG 10

Fixing one's eyes upon the tip of one's nose is called Nāsāgra-Dṛṣṭi in Saṅskṛta. Nāsāgra means the tip of the nose and Dṛṣṭi means gaze. It is illustrated in Fig. 10. It may be practised as a part of Padmāsana or independent of it. In the accompanying picture, the head is thrown a little backward with a view to make the position of the eyeballs visible.

The Nasal Gaze is a fine exercise for the wandering mind. Its practice, if undertaken with zest and carried over a period of some months continuously, has a perceptibly beneficial effect upon the unsteady mind.

Caution - The Nasal Gaze directly works upon the brain through the optic nerves. Everybody should, therefore, develop this gaze very slowly and cautiously. Persons with weak nerves are warned not to undertake this practice except under expert supervision.

Bhrūmadhya-Dṛṣṭi or The Frontal Gaze

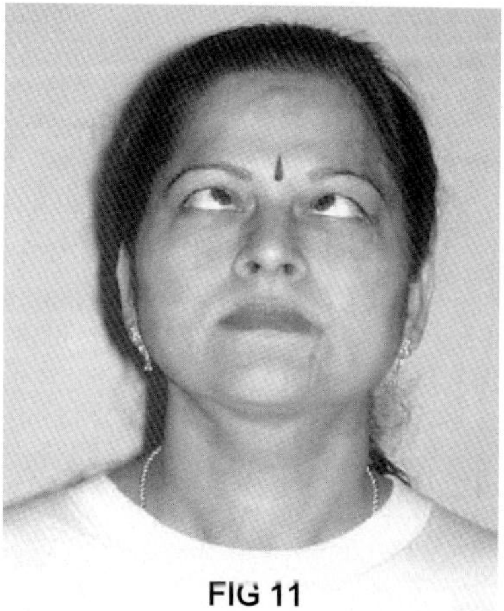

FIG 11

Fixing one's eyes between the eyebrows is called Bhrūmadhya-Dṛṣṭi in Saṅskṛta, Bhrūmadhya means the space between the eyebrows. This Dṛṣṭi is illustrated in Fig. 11. It may be practised as a part of Siddhāsana[1] or independent of it.

Like the Nasal Gaze, the Frontal Gaze is a fine exercise for the mind. But the advice and caution given in the case of the former are equally applicable to the case of the latter. Hence they should be carefully borne in mind by the enthusiastic student of Yoga.

1. Described later on in this chapter.

Uḍḍiyāna-Bandha or The Raising of the Diaphragm

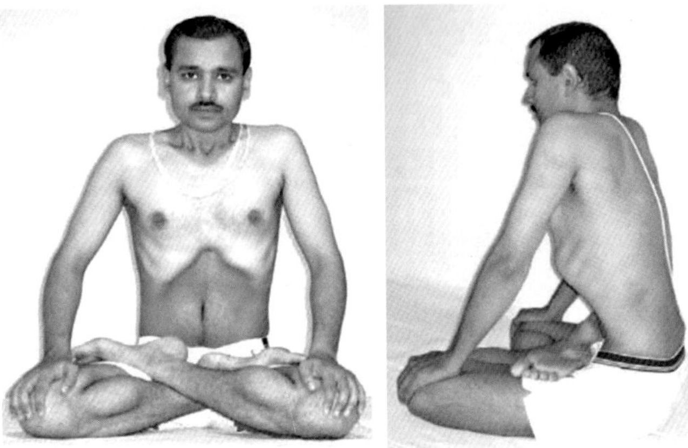

FIG 12

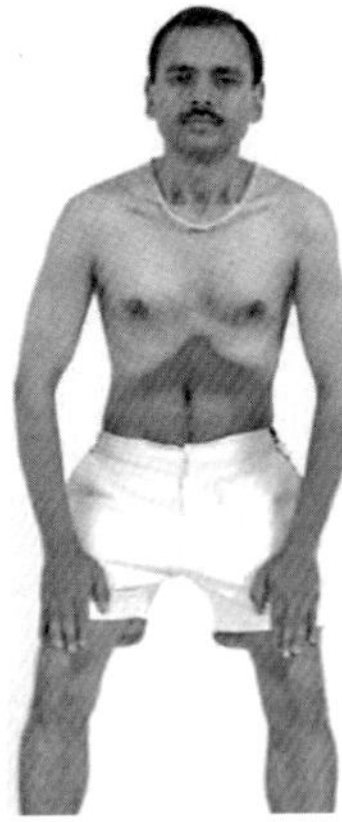

FIG 13

Uḍḍiyāna is an exercise of the diaphragm and the ribs. When expressed in a popular[1] language its technique may be described as follows :

As this Bandha is practised either in sitting or in standing, the student poses himself as shown in Fig. 12 and 13 respectively. In these pictures, hands are shown to be resting either on the knees or on the thighs. This position of the hands enables them to be firmly pressed against their support and thus to fix up the muscles of the neck and the shoulders. Having taken this posture the student secures the deepest possible expiration by vigorously contracting the front muscles of the abdomen. The chest also stands contracted. While the breath is held out, the muscles of the neck and the shoulders are fixed up by firmly pressing the hands either against the knees or against the thighs as the case may be. Then a vigorous mock inhalation is attempted by raising the ribs and by not allowing the air to flow into the lungs. Simultaneously the front abdominal muscles are completely relaxed.

---

1. This Bandha has been subjected by us to a very large number of X-ray and other experiments, many of which have already appeared in Yoga-Mīmāṁsā. Hence we are in a position to give a detailed scientific description of its technique. Looking to the popular character of this publication however, we have sketched its technique in the simplest terms possible.

The fixing up of the neck and shoulders, the vigorous mock inhalation preceded by the deepest possible exhalation and the simultaneous relaxation of the contracted front abdominal muscles, these three actions complete the technique of Uḍḍiyāna. Automatically[1] the diaphragm will rise up and the abdomen will undergo pronounced depression, producing the concave appearance shown in Figs. 12 and 13. A slight forward bent of the trunk will be helpful in securing greater abdominal concavity. This position is required to be maintained throughout the exercise of Uḍḍiyāna.

When the student finds that he can no longer hold his breath out comfortably, he relaxes his neck and shoulders, lets go the ribs and slowly starts inhalation, allowing the abdominal depression to be effaced gradually. When inhalation is completed, one round of the Uḍḍiyāna exercise is finished.

In Saṅskṛta, Uḍḍiyāna means raising up and Bandha means contraction of particular anatomical parts. This exercise is called Uddiyāna Bandha because the muscular contractions described above enable the spiritual force[2] to rise up. Anatomically this Bandha may be called Uḍḍiyāna because it raises the diaphragm.

Uḍḍiyāna is a very fine exercise of the abdomen. Its therapeutical value against constipation, dyspepsia, liver troubles etc., is very great. Its spiritual worth is greater still.

Caution - People suffering from circulatory or serious abdominal troubles should not take to this exercise on their own responsibility.

---

1. The pressure changes in the chest and abdomen which are responsible for this automatic abdominal depression, have been detailed in Yoga-Mīmāṁsā in places too numerous to be quoted here. Zealous students of Yogic physiology may read the Scientific Sections of Vols. II and IV of that journal.

2. This force is locked up in the lower region of the abdomen. Uḍḍiyāna is one of the different exercises capable of letting loose this force and making it to travel upward along the spine.

Jālandhara-Bandha or The Chin-Lock

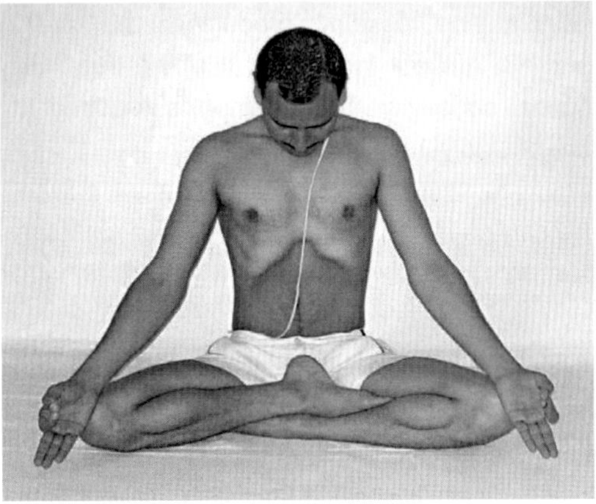

FIG 14

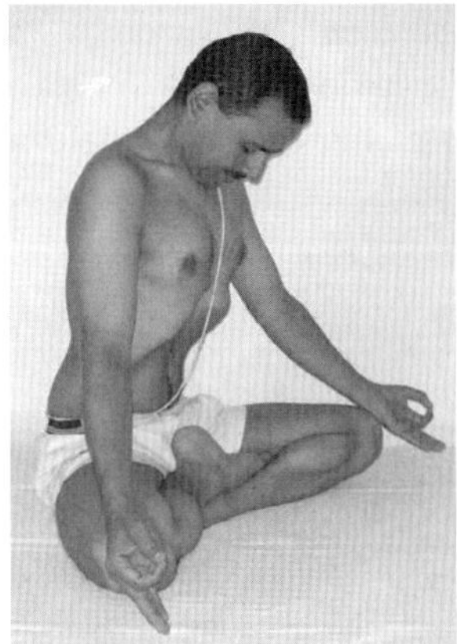

FIG 15

Jālandhara-Bandha requires the chin to be closely pressed against the chest. For doing this the chin is to be tightly set in the jugular notch with the necessary bent of the neck and the head. This has been shown in the pictures of Padmāsana and Siddhāsana given in this book later on. According to some traditions, however, the chin is not set in the jugular notch but pressed against the chest further down about four fingers below it. Figs. 14 and 15 illustrate this.

The Chin-Lock may be practised as a part of Padmāsana and Siddhāsana or independent of them.

This Bandha exercise an upward pull upon the spine and most probably upon the spinal cord, and thus works upon the brain. The Yogic tradition traces the name Jālandhara-Bandha to these circumstances: The word Jāla referring to the brain and to the nerves passing through the neck, and Dhara denoting the upward pull. Is it possible for the name of the Bandha to be taken from the great Yogin Jālandhara, who was, perhaps, its inventor, or, at any rate, its famous exponent?

Mūla-Bandha or The Anal Contraction

FIG 18

Mūla-Bandha is an exercise which mainly consists in forcibly contracting the anal sphincters. It also requires the perineum to be closely pressed by the heel, as illustrated in Fig. 18 and as described later on in this chapter in the technique of Siddhāsana.

Mūla-Bandha may be practised as a part of Siddhāsana or independent of it.

There are two anal sphincters, one internal and the other external, situated at the end of the rectum. Both the sphincters, are formed by circular muscles, the external one constituting the anus.

Although the anal contraction alone goes to form Mūla-Bandha is intended to work upon the central and sympathetic nervous systems through the nerve terminals in the anal sphincters. It is called Mūla Bandha because it first concerns itself with the lower ends of the nervous system in the human trunk.

Caution - A mistake in the practice of this Bandha leads to hard constipation and upsets the digestive system. The genitals are also involved in this contraction and a mistake in its execution may result in some trouble in that direction also. Hence students of Yoga are advised to proceed systematically into this practice.

Padmāsana or The Lotus Pose

FIG 16

FIG 17

THE NAME:

The pose is called Padmāsana because it is in imitation of the lotus that the hands and feet are arranged in this Āsana. Padma, in Sanskṛta, means a lotus. Possibly the two feet placed on the opposite thighs represent the lotus leaves, and the two hands arranged one above to other stand for the blooming lotus. Fig. 17 illustrates the full pose.

THE TECHNIQUE:

The student first takes his seat with his legs fully stretched out. He then bends his right leg in the knee-joint; and folding it upon itself, sets the same in the root of the thigh with its sole upturned. (vide Fig. 16). The other leg is similarly folded and set in the opposite hip-joint. Both the heels he adjusts in such a way that they almost meet in front of the pubic bones and each of them presses on the abdominal portion adjacent to it. (vide Fig. 17). Then on the heels thighs brought together, the left hand is spread out with its back touching the heels and its palm upturned. The right hand is placed upon the left in the same manner. The eyes are directed to the nose-tip as described on p. 51; and the chin lock is formed after the manner indicated on p. 55. With the Anal Contraction treated on p. 56, the technique of the Lotus Pose is complete. It is needless to add that except for the neck, the spine is to be maintained erect.

The most important features of Padmāsana are the two Bandhas - Jālandhara and Mūla. As these are to be cautiously practised, it is always desirable, for the student of Yoga, first to pick up the Bandhas and then start with this pose.

Caution - In India many people are desirous of sitting in Padmāsana for their daily prayers. We advise these people to assume the Lotus Pose without the Bandhas, if they have not already picked them up successfully. When practised without Bandhas, this Āsana may be continued for any length of time, provided one can sit in it all the while without any sense of discomfort. The advice and caution given in the notes on the Jālandhara and Mūla Bandhas, also hold good in the case of Padmāsana, if the student is anxious to go through the complete technique of this posture.

CULTURAL ADVANTAGES:

All over the lower extremities, the flexors are greatly contracted and pressed.

This circumstance coupled with the passive condition of all the remaining muscles of the lower extremities maintained for a considerably long time, interferes with the free current of blood circulation. That being the case, the pelvic region gets larger blood supply from the bifurcation of the abdominal aorta.

The larger blood supply mentioned above tones up the coccygeal and sacral nerves.

The same advantages can be claimed for all the meditative poses that follow.

Siddhāsana or The Accomplished Pose

FIG18

FIG19

THE NAME:

The pose is called Siddhāsana because it is a favourite pose of the accomplished Yogins. Sidha, in Saṅskṛta, means an adept.

THE TECHNIQUE:

The student first takes his seat with his legs fully stretched out. He then bends his left leg in the knee-joint; and folding it upon itself, sets its heel tightly against the perineum. (vide Fig.18). In order to get the perineum clear for this purpose, he has first to hold up his genitals with the left hand, for the right hand is occupied in setting the heel in its proper place. The sole of the left foot should be closely in touch with the right thigh. No attempt should be made to sit on the heel. This is a wrong procedure, because pressure is to be exerted on the perineum and not on the anus. The adjusted heel should feel the hard touch of the bones on the two sides of the perineum. After the left leg is given its proper position, the genitals should be arranged within the space available between the left thigh and the left calf. This being done the right leg should be folded after the manner of the left, its heel being placed against the pubic bones just above the penis. (vide Fig. 19). The right sole should spread along the left thigh, the lower border of the right foot being thrust between the left thigh and the left calf. Care must be taken not to hurt the genitals. Generally they can be accommodated below the right heel. But if they cannot find sufficient space there, the testes may be lodged there and the penis may be made to lie outside the folded legs. Under no circumstances undesirable pressure should be put upon any of the organs concerned.

The chin is set against the chest, just as in Padmāsana, to form Jālandhara-Bandha. The eyes, this time, do not, however, gaze at the tip of the nose; but are directed between the eyebrows, as described on page 52, securing Bhrūmadhya-Dṛṣṭi for the student. Except for this bent of the neck required to form Jālandhara-Bandha, the spine is to be kept erect.

The hands and fingers may be arranged to form Jñāna-Mudrā[1] as shown in Fig. 18 or the hands may rest on the knees, touching them with their palms.

The pose should be developed gradually every possibility of uncomfortable pressure. The period of time given to its daily practice should increase slowly.

Note - In some of the vernacular books of Yoga, the pose is said to affect the sexual powers adversely. So far as our experience goes, there is little evidence in support of this view, in the case of healthy persons. It is, however, desirable not to exceed an hour's practice, without special permission of an expert.

This and the preceding Āsana are principally practised for spiritual culture. When rightly advised they are also available for purposes of physical culture and therapeutics.

1. Jñāna-Mudrā or the Symbol of knowledge is practised in the following manner. The palms are fully stretched and the tip of the index finger, that is, the finger next to the thumb, is made to touch the tip of the thumb of the same hand. In this action, it is forefinger that is bent to meet the thumb, the latter advancing a little, no doubt, to meet its fellow.

Svastikāsana or The Auspicious Pose

FIG 20

FIG 21

THE NAME:

The pose is called Svastikāsana because it involved crossing of the legs which is looked upon by the Āryanas as auspicious. In Saṅskṛta, svastika means auspicious. In classical Saṅskṛta the word Svastika is used even for the crossing of the hands. The reason is that mysterious symbol is mainly represented by two lines crossing each other at right angles. Hence positions involving the crossing either of hands or of legs are also called Svastika. Fig. 21 which illustrates Svastikāsana, clearly how in this Āsana legs cross each other above the ankles.

THE TECHNIQUE:

The student starts by stretching out his legs on his seat. Then he bends one of his legs, say the right, in the knee, and folds it on the thigh, just as in the case of Siddhāsana. But there is difference in the ultimate position of the foot in this pose and in Siddhāsana. In the latter pose the heel is set against the perineum, whereas in Svastikāsana it is to be set against the opposite hip-joint, so as to allow the corresponding sole to be in close touch with the opposite thigh. (vide Fig. 20). Then without disturbing the position of the heel, the student raises the toes of his right leg with his left hand. Simultaneously he folds his left leg upon the thigh in such a way that the big toe of his right leg may project itself above the calf and the thigh between which it is held, and the left heel may be firmly set against the right hip-joint. The toes of the left foot are inserted between the right calf and the right thigh already folded upon each other, allowing only the big left toe to lie free. (vide Fig. 21). Needless to say that in this position the sole of the left foot stretches above the right thigh touching it closely all along. In this pose the legs should be made to cross each other just above the ankles, so that all unpleasant pressure on the bones will be avoided. When the legs are properly adjusted a sort of foot-lock is prepared which one finds very comfortable, and capable of being maintained for a considerable length of time.

The spine is to be kept erect. No attempt is, however, to be made to throw out the chest. Svastikāsana is a meditative pose and as such requires to be maintained for a long time. Any attempt to give an artificial bent to the vertebral column is likely to involve a strain.

The arms may hang loosely from the shoulders and rest on the knees covering them with their palms. Or they may be stretched out a little further so as to allow the wrist to rest on the corresponding knees. In the latter case, the hands are formed into what is called Jñāna-Mudrā in Yoga. Fig. 21 illustrates the full pose.

The third way of arranging the hands is shown in Padmāsana. (vide Fig. 17).

Instead of starting with the right leg, the student may start with the left. He might then go through the whole technique, introducing corresponding changes throughout.

The eyes may either be closed as illustrated in Fig. 21 or either the Nasal Gaze or the Frontal Gaze or the Frontal Gaze may be practised. (For the two Dṛṣṭi see respectively (Fig. 10 and 11).

Samāsana
or The Symmetrical Pose

FIG 22

FIG 23

THE NAME:

The pose is called Samāsana because in its performance all the parts of the human body are symmetrically arranged and a perfect balance is maintained. In Saṅskṛta, Sama means symmetrical.

Guptāsana is another name given to this pose. In Saṅskṛta, Gupta means either well protected or secret. The pose looks to be called Guptāsana because in executing it, genitals are well protected under the heels of man. Or it may be that the Āsana was practised secretly by a particular school of Yogins and continued to be their secret possession, till it became known to others and hence acquired this name.

THE TECHNIQUE:

The only difference in the technique of this Āsana and the previous one, lies in the arrangement of the heels. In Svastikāsana the right heel is pressed against the opposite groin and also the left. But in Samāsana the right and the left heels are to be set against the pubic bones. This is done as follows. While the right leg is being folded on the corresponding thigh, the student holds the heels in his right hand and the toes in his left. Then he turns the heel upward and the toes downward, and arranges the foot in his front in such a way that the heel presses against the pubic bones, the sole is turned upwards, and the upper surface of the foot touches the ground. (vide Fig. 22). Care must be taken at this time to see that the genitals are placed below the heel in such a way that no pressure is exerted on the testes. The other leg is similarly folded, and the other heel is placed upon the first heel, pressing against the pubic bones. The toes of the other leg are to be inserted between the calf and the thigh of the first leg. (vide Fig 23).

The arrangement of the hands and eyes in this Āsana admits of as many varieties as in the previous Āsana. The spine is to be maintained erect and the whole body to be kept in balance.

Note - as in this pose the space below the heels in just sufficient to accommodate genitals of the normal size, persons who are suffering from hydrocele etc., should not attempt this Āsana.

4
CULTURAL POSES

Śīrṣāsana
Sarvāṅgāsana
Matsyāsana
Halāsana
Bhujaṅgāsana
Śalabhāsana
Ardha-Śalabhāsana
Dhanurāsana
Ardha-Matsyendrāsana
Vakrāsana
Siṃhāsana
Vajrāsana
Supta-Vajrāsana
Paśchimatāna
Mayūrāsana
Śavāsana

Śīrṣāsana or

FIG 24

THE NAME:

The pose is called Śīrṣāsana because it requires the student to stand on the head. Śīrṣā means the head in Saṅskṛta, and Āsana means a Yogic pose.

THE TECHNIQUE:

To begin with the student kneels on his seat and prepares a finger-lock by pushing the fingers of his right hand between those of the left till their roots are well-knit together. Then in his front, he makes a convenient angle with his forearms, the finger-lock serving as the vertex. (vide Fig. 24). Then he places his head at the vertex. For this purpose the hinder part of the head is to be used and not the part nearer the forehead. The reason is that during the balanced condition, as illustrated in Figs. 25 to 30, the spine must stand as erect as possible, so that it can easily bear the burden of the whole body. If the front part is employed the spine would suffer a curve in the cervical region and put an unnecessary strain upon it. All this time the student is kneeling on his seat as shown in Fig. 24. After this he slowly raises his trunk lifting up the lower end of it, and tries to hold it perpendicular to the ground. For this purpose he puts the weight of his trunk on three points; the two elbows and the head supported by the finger lock. He gradually raises his knees and brings his toes nearer to his face. When the trunk supported on the head is sufficiently thrown backward, the student finds that he could lift his toes from the ground without standing in danger of a collapse. (vide Fig. 25). All these movements he accomplishes very smoothly and does not give any jerks to his body, for they are likely to upset the balance rather than establish it.

The Topsyturvy Pose

FIG 25 FIG 26 FIG 27 FIG 28

He then draws his knees to his chest, folds his legs, straightens his back, and tries to be firm in his balance in this position. (vide Fig. 26). The practice of this first stage of Śīrṣāsana is continued over some days, so that the muscles get used to it and their work becomes easy.

When the student can do this first part of the Āsana with ease and grace, his remaining task is very simple. In the second stage, he is simply to straighten out his thighs and bring them in a line with the trunk. (vide Fig. 27). Here the balance is never allowed to go to the back side. The whole work is smoothly accomplished by contracting the muscles of the back and the buttocks. The third and the last stage is reached when the legs are opened out; and the whole frame stands at right angles to the ground. (vide Fig. 28).

Just as ordinarily we do not feel the slightest burden of our body on any part of it, while we are standing on the legs, so by practice, the student, in this pose, does not experience any burden, as the whole body stands perfectly balanced, and the weight is evenly distributed over its different parts.

The balance required for Śīrṣāsana is best secured by the methods indicated in the last three paragraphs. People look to be under impression that they could get somebody to hold them up in the air; or failing the services of an intelligent living being, even if they could get a dead wall for support. The legs are tossed with violent jerks, and these hasty people often find themselves playing the part of a tumbler, only minus his acrobatic skill! Even if they fare better, the psychological need of a support continues to be felt all along and these persons always feel insecure in this posture, even after months of daily practice. But students who try to go without any outside help from the very beginning, obtain the necessary skill in a few days.

After maintaining the Āsana across the necessary length of time, the student returns to his normal position by retracing the same steps through which he attains the full pose.

Great care must be taken about the period to be devoted to this practice. The best way is to start with 15 seconds and to increase the time very cautiously. Every symptom should be watched and the least possibility of overdoing one's part be avoided. If proper precautions are taken, there is absolutely nothing in this pose which might lead to trouble. The maximum period should be 24 minutes. We have seen, however, a number of people practising this Āsana for more than half an hour every day, and thereby maintaining very sound health. Some of these are past fifty, and in their communications addressed to us, bear eloquent testimony to the manifold advantages a regular practice of this pose can give.

The maximum of 24 minutes mentioned in the last paragraph has been prescribed for the pose when it is practiced by itself. If Śīrṣāsana is undertaken as a part of the daily Yogic exercises, the longest time should be devoted to it is only twelve minutes.

LIMITATIONS:

Although Śīrṣāsana is available to every man of average health, there are particular limitations which require careful attention. These limitations are as enumerated below.

1. People suffering from aching or running ears should avoid Śīrṣāsana.
2. The pose is contra-indicated not only during the time when the disease is active, but even for some time after the trouble has subsided.
3. Persons having weak eye capillaries should avoid Śīrṣāsana. If, however, these eye capillaries are strengthened by other exercises, Śīrṣāsana would be available afterwards.
4. Individuals recording blood pressure above 150 and below 100 mm, Hg. habitually, should not take to Śīrṣāsana on their own responsibility. They should consult an expert.

5. Persons with a weak heart should practise Śīrṣāsana very cautiously. If standing on the head sets up palpitations the pose should be definitely avoided.
6. Serious cases of chronic nasal catarrh are made worse by the practice of Śīrṣāsana. In the initial stage, however, nasal catarrh can be effectively treated by means of this pose.
7. Constipated persons passing excessively dry stool should avoid Śīrṣāsana.
8. The practice of Śīrṣāsana should never be undertaken immediately after any violent exercise. At least twenty minutes should be allowed to go by.

CULTURAL ADVANTAGES:

All the activities of man, whether mental or physical, are governed from the brain. The whole nervous system which spreads throughout the body like a network of wires, is directly or indirectly connected with this organ. When a man stands on his head he sends a richer supply of the arterial blood to the brain and thus maintains the health of not only the brain itself, but of the whole nervous system.

The organs of the sense of sight, smell, hearing and taste depend for their efficient functioning upon the different centres situated in the brain. Śīrṣāsana exercises a very beneficial influence upon the health of these centres and preserves the efficiency of the sense organs.

Some of the most important endocrine glands are situated above the heart. When a man stands upside-down these glands are richly supplied with the fresh blood and their health is promoted. The pineal gland and the pituitary body get the greatest advantage. The thyroid and the parathyroid have also their share in this advantage; but it is not so large.

Organs of digestion are immediately benefited because of Śīrṣāsana. The blood circulating through these organs passes to the liver through the portal vein, which in its turn drains it into the inferior vena cava. In the Topsyturvy pose this portal circulation of the venous blood is very greatly helped because of the inverted position of the body. It is a general physiological rule that an organ which can satisfactory drain its venous blood gets a rich supply of the fresh blood from the arteries. The portal circulation of the venous blood being satisfactorily established, the organs of digestion get a richer supply of the arterial blood, and are made healthier for it.

Thus it will be seen that Śīrṣāsana beneficially influences the health of the nervous system, of the endocrine system, and of the digestive system, the last including the organs of excretion. As the general well-being of an individual depends upon the satisfactory functioning of the systems mentioned just now, Śīrṣāsana is a very great help in maintaining one's general health and promoting organic vigour.

THERAPEUTICAL ADVANTAGES:

Under **CULTURAL ADVANTAGES** we have said that Śīrṣāsana favorably influences the nervous, the endocrine and the digestive systems. Now if any of these systems go out of order diseases arise. These diseases, under particular circumstances, can be treated with Śīrṣāsana.

NEURASTHENIA - This is a disease developing out of the degeneration of nerves. The symptoms which mark this disease are lack of energy, a sense of fullness and pressure at the top of the head, easy fatigue, dullness, failure of memory, want of sleep, dyspepsia and constipation. All these symptoms are due to one cause, the degeneration of nerve-centres. Now as all the nerve-centres are directly or indirectly connected with the brain, these systems can be treated by treating the brain by means of Śīrṣāsana.

DYSPEPSIA & CONSTIPATION - These two diseases develop when the organs of digestion go out of order. If the digestive disorder is due to defective blood circulation or to the degenerated nervous mechanism, it can be set right by means of Śīrṣāsana.

CONGESTED THROAT - Congestion in the throat, especially if it is due to dyspeptic conditions can be relieved by Śīrṣāsana.

CONGESTED LIVER & SPLEEN - The liver and the spleen very often become congested. This congestion can be relieved by establishing free blood circulation in these organs by means of Śīrṣāsana.

VISCEROPTOSIS - Due to the weakness of the abdominal muscles and consequent presence of constipation, the abdominal viscera have a tendency to drop into the pelvic region. This disease is known as visceroptosis. The trouble can be considerably counteracted by Śīrṣāsana.

HERNIA - This disease can be effectively checked in its incipient stage and may be kept under fair control even after it has established itself. When Śīrṣāsana is being practised for a cure of hernia, great care must be taken to get the technique of the pose modified according to the needs of the individual. For this modification expert advice is imperative.

SEMINAL WEAKNESS - Due to the situation of the seminal sacks between the bladder and the rectum, frequently nocturnal discharges take place in the latter part of the night, because both the bladder and the rectum happen to be loaded during these hours especially in the case of constipated people. These discharges can be checked by the practice of Śīrṣāsana.

Many people suffer from the trouble of premature ejaculations and also of wet dreams, because their genitals are congested with the venous blood. When this is the case, Śīrṣāsana is found to be of great help.

ASTHMA - Śīrṣāsana can be taken advantage of in the cure of particular types of asthma, especially of the nervous and hepatic types.

FURTHER DEVELOPMENTS OF ŚĪRṢĀSANA:

The different stages through which the full Topsyturvy Pose can be attained, have been stated up to now. When the Yogic culturist practises this Āsana for some days, he gets a complete control of his body and finds himself so thoroughly balanced that he can throw his limbs into different folds and twists, without fearing a collapse, although he continues to stand on the head all the while. Then it is time for him to go into the further development.

FIRST DEVELOPMENT

FIG 29

THE TECHNIQUE:

Instead of keeping the legs erect, they are to be folded into a foot-lock. This constitutes the first development. For this purpose the student bends one of his legs, preferably the right, in the knee-joint; and folding it upon the right thigh, sets the same in the opposite hip-joint, so that the right heel lies at the root of the left thigh and the upturned sole stretches itself along the same towards the knee. (vide Fig. 29). One may find it difficult to secure this adjustment at once. In that case the right foot might be set anywhere on the opposite thigh, and then slided down to the required position with the help of muscle contraction, the upper part of the contracted foot all the while pressing upon the thigh.

During this attempt the student should maintain his balance throwing the weight of his legs a little to the front, so that he would find it easier to recover it, should he chance to lose the same in his movements. It is our common experience that we are generally able to save ourselves from a fall, should we tend to fall forward; but we are sure to come to the ground, should we lose our balance in the opposite direction. This is because a tendency to fall forward is counteracted by the back muscles of the legs, as they immediately begin to act from the foot, which by its contraction and adjustment gives a good support to the legs. In a backward fall, however, there is no support, and the balance, once lost, can rarely be regained. The same principle applies to Śīrṣāsana. The head and the forearms resting on the ground from a good support for the whole body; and taking the place of the foot in our ordinary standing, save the Yogic culturist from a forward fall. Here the muscles of the upper extremities and the thorax act just as the muscles of the legs in our usual standing position. But a tendency to fall backward can scarcely be checked; because there is nothing that can effectively support the head from behind. The finger-lock offers little help in this respect.

When the right foot is properly set in its place, the left leg is bent in the knee and similarly adjusted in the right hip-joint. This completes the first development. The whole spine stands erect and the foot-lock is held in a line with the trunk.

Now this foot-lock is characteristic of Padmāsana, and as the foot-lock is held aloft in this development of Śīrṣāsana (vide Fig. 29). This development is known as Utthitordhva Padmāsana (meaning Hoisted Padmāsana). in Yogic literature Utthita means raised and Ūrdhva means aloft in Saṅskṛta.

SECOND DEVELOPMENT

FIG 30

FIG 31

After maintaining the foot-lock straight for a while, the student folds it upon his abdomen through the hip-joint. (vide Fig. 30). When the folded legs touch the abdomen, the foot-lock is slided down along the thorax to the armpits. This part of the Āsana is accomplished by throwing into powerful contractions the abdominal muscles and vigorously stretching the back muscles and the spine.

THIRD DEVELOPMENT

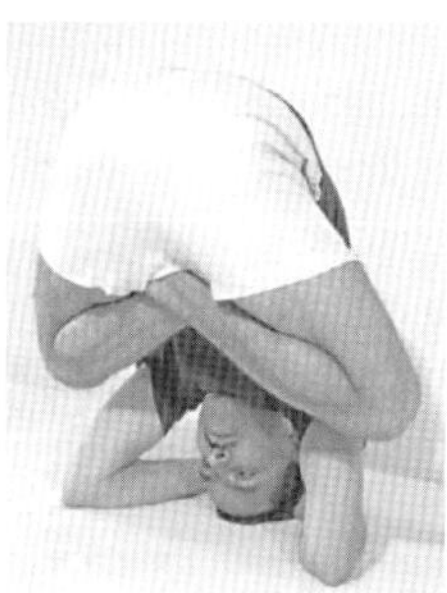

FIG 32

The third and the last development is reached, when the trunk is flexed upon the arms, through the shoulder-joints, the foot-lock still resting in the armpits. The whole body is folded in almost every important joint and is thrown, as it were, into a knot! (vide Fig. 32). The whole spine and the back from a regular curve and the abdominal muscles experience the most vigorous contraction.

NOTE:

At times the student starts his Śīrṣāsana not with his free legs, but with his legs folded in a lock. (For the method of forming a foot-lock, read Matsyāsana). In that case he reaches the third development first; and then going through the second and first developments, he ultimately unfolds his foot-lock and holds his lower extremities straight in the air to attain the full pose of Śīrṣāsana. It will be seen that procedure merely reverses the different stages described in the technique and further developments of Śīrṣāsana in the foregoing pages.

When this procedure is followed the student has to start with a foot-lock and has to take Utthitordhva Padmāsana before attaining the full pose of Śīrṣāsana.

CULTURAL ADVANTAGES:

These three developments of Śīrṣāsana constitute an excellent exercise for the deep and superficial muscles of the back as well as for the muscles of the abdomen. While standing on the head, these developments may be traced and retraced; and when this folding and unfolding is repeated several times, all the muscles of the trunk are alternately contracted and relaxed.

THERAPEUTICAL ADVANTAGES:

These developments are somewhat strenuous and should not be taken advantage of in therapeutical work.

Sarvāṅgāsana or The Pan-Physical Pose

THE NAME:

The pose is called Sarvāṅgāsana because it influences the thyroid and through it the whole body and its functions. In Saṅskṛta, Sarva means the whole and Aṅga means the body.

THE TECHNIQUE:

The student first lies supine on his seat with all muscles completely relaxed as shown in Fig. 33. Then he slowly raises his legs through the hip-joint till they make an angle of 30 degrees with the ground. Here the legs are kept steady for a few seconds, and then raised through another 30 degrees. Again they are kept steady here and again raised so as to complete right angle. This is maintained for a few seconds again.[1]

Up to now the student does not bring into action his arms and elbows which play only a passive part. But here he raises his whole body with his legs thrown up; and resting his weight on his arms, assumes the position shown in Figs 34 and 35. At this point the student must see that his chest presses against his chin forming what has already been described as the Chin-Lock. (vide p. 55). Further, in order to render the Chin-Lock perfect, he bends his forearms through the elbows and with his hands presses his trunk against the chin, until it is well set in the jugular notch. Fig. 36 represents the full pose, and Fig. 37 gives the back view of it. In this practice the posterior part of the neck lies close along the ground, the trunk and the legs are in a straight line and the mind is fixed on the thyroid. Only under exceptional circumstances attention is directed to the toes as shown in Fig. 36.

According to some traditions Sarvāṅgāsana is completed by raising the trunk while the hands remain extended, as illustrated in Figs. 34 and 35.

This may be looked upon as a mere variation of Sarvāṅgāsana as we have described it above; and may be called Sarvāṅgāsana with Hands Extended.

---

1. These stages have not been prescribed in the Yogic texts, nor are they required by different Yogic traditions. They are included here as they can be easily developed while raising the legs through a right angle, and as they posses cultural and curative values.

FIG 33

If Sarvāṅgāsana is to be practised by itself, the maximum time to be devoted to it should be twenty-four minutes, out of which four minutes may be given to the variation noticed in the last paragraph. Six minutes should be sufficient for the practice of Sarvāṅgāsana when it forms only a part of the daily exercises. In this case the variation may be safely omitted.

CULTURAL ADVANTAGES:

The principal cultural advantage of Sarvāṅgāsana lies in the maintenance of a healthy thyroid. As is well-known this gland is responsible for the general health of an individual. By taking care of the thyroid, Sarvāṅgāsana is able to maintain the whole human organism in a healthy condition.

The difference between Śīrṣāsana and Sarvāṅgāsana lies in the position of the head. In both the poses the remaining part of the body stands vertical to the ground. Hence the cultural advantages that accrue from Śīrṣāsana due to the vertical position of the body, are also secured in Sarvāṅgāsana. The Pan-physical Pose very beneficially influences the sex glands both in males and females.

THERAPEUTICAL ADVANTAGES:

Symptoms of old age due to the faulty functioning of the thyroid are counteracted by means of Sarvāṅgāsana. Seminal weakness arising from the degeneration of the testes in the case of males and sexual disorders arising from

the degeneration of the ovaries in the females can be extensively controlled by the practice of Sarvāṅgāsana. Dyspepsia, constipation, hernia, visceroptosis can be treated by Sarvāṅgāsana as well as by Śīrṣāsana.

FIG 34

FIG 35

FIG 36

FIG 37

Matsyāsana or

FIG 38

FIG 39

THE NAME:

The pose called Matsyāsana because in swimming a person can float on water, like the fish, for a considerable time, if he steadily lies there in this posture. In Saṅskṛta Matsya means the fish.

THE TECHNIQUE:

The student first takes his seat with his legs fully stretched out as shown in Fig. 38. He then bends one of his legs, preferably the right, in the knee-joint; and folding it upon itself, sets the same in the opposite hip-joint, so as to allow the foot to lie stretching at the root of the thigh with its sole turned upward. The other leg is similarly folded and set in the opposite hip-joint. Both the heels he adjusts in such a way that each of them presses on the adjacent portion of the abdomen. This forms the foot-lock shown in Figs 39 and 40. Fig. 39 represents this foot-lock folded on the abdomen at right angles as is done in sitting posture. Fig. 40 shows the same unfolded and held straight line with the abdomen. After forming the foot-lock the student lies supine on his seat. Then resting his weight on the elbows, he raises his trunk and head; and throwing the latter backward with an arched spine makes a bridge on his seat. (vide Fig . 41). Subsequently he makes hooks of his forefingers and with these takes hold of the opposite toes which are now available on thoir wrong sides. Fig. 42 gives the front view of the pose Very often the hands instead of being given the position described above, are folded round the head.

The Fish Pose

FIG 40 FIG 41

The practice of Matsyāsana cannot be neglected if one wants to reap the full benefits of Sarvāṅgāsana, as the former pose forms a necessary complement of the latter. When thus undertaken Matsyāsana should be given only 3/10 of the time devoted to the main pose.

CULTURAL & THERAPEUTICAL ADVANTAGES:

This pose is to be practised as complementary to Sarvāṅgāsana. It greatly helps an individual to ensure the benefits he would get from the practice of Sarvāṅgāsana, so far as the thyroid is concerned.

FIG 42

Halāsana or

FIG 43

FIG 44

THE NAME:

The pose is called Halāsana in its practice the body is made to imitate the shape of the Indian plough. Hala means a plough in Saṅskṛta.

THE TECHNIQUE:

To start with the student lies supine on his seat as in the case of Sarvāṅgāsana . (vide Fig. 33). Then he slowly raises his legs through the hip-joint until they make an angle of 30 degrees with the ground. Here the legs are kept steady for a few seconds; and then raised through another 30 degrees. Again they are kept steady here and again raised so as to complete a right angle. This is maintained for a few seconds again. This part of the Plough Pose may be called Ardha-Halāsana[1].

After this the student keeps his trunk, as far as possible, close to the ground; and only bends his legs further, raising his hips and the lower part of his back only as much as is needed for securing the first stage of the pose as illustrated in Fig. 43. This is done as follows: The legs that were carried through an angle of 90 degrees, are lowered on the side of the head, so much so that the toes are made to touch the ground beyond the head. They are, however, kept nearest to the head; and the whole pressure of the hips and the thighs is thrown

1. These stages have not been prescribed in the Yogic texts, nor are they required by different Yogic traditions. They are included here as they can be easily developed while raising the legs through a right angle; and are helpful in developing abdominal muscles and in relieving constipation.

The Plough Pose

FIG 45

FIG 46

on the lumbosacral region of the spine. During this as well as the next two stages, the hands are not allowed to change their extended and passive position. As usual the leg movement are accomplished smoothly and steadily. If the full curve necessary for reaching the first stage in Halāsana cannot be secured at the very first attempt, it should be attained bit by bit everyday. Fig. 43 gives the side view of this first stage of Halāsana.

When this stage has been maintained for a few seconds, the toes are pushed farther from the head, until the pressure is felt at the lower dorsal region of the spinal curve. This constitutes the second stage, and is represented in Fig. 44.

After a few seconds pause here, the toes are again slided further away, until at last the farthest point is reached, and the burden is thrown on the upper dorsal part of the spinal curve. This is shown in Fig. 45, and constitutes the third stage of Halāsana.

A few seconds in the third stage, and the student prepares himself for the final stage in Halāsana. The hands which up to now played only a passive part, are withdrawn from their places; and after being taken beyond the head, are there made to form a finger lock[1]. This finger-lock is placed just near the head and the toes are pushed back again, until the pressure is experienced at the cervical part of the spinal curve. This arrangement of the body presses the chest so tightly upon the chin that a perfect Chin-Lock is effected. (vide Fig. 46). Here the technique of Halāsana is completed.

1. The technique of this lock has been explained under Śīrṣāsana.

With a view to contrast the different stage of this Āsana they have all been grouped together in Fig. 48, which gives the back view of the same.

In recovering the original position the following method is to be followed.

First the fingers are unlocked and the hands are restored to their original extended position. After this the toes are drawn nearer the head and all the steps that were previously taken are gone through in the reverse order, until at last, the student lies supine on his seat as he originally did.

NOTE:

For the purposes of physical culture it is desirable to repeat the practice rather than to maintain the different stages of the pose for a long time in one and the same attempt. This does not apply to spiritual culture, which requires the first stage to be kept up for a considerably long time. It is to be remembered that for spiritual culture the other three stages are of little use.

Halāsana when it is being practised as a part of the Short Course, should be devoted two seconds in each of the stages through which either the legs are carried or the spine is curved. But when the pose is being practised as a part of the Full Course, each stage should be given three seconds except the final, which may be given half a minute to itself. It will take six turns of Halāsana to cover to the four minutes, maximum prescribed for this pose.

As an item of the Easy Course only Ardha-Halāsana is available and is to be developed as shown in Appendix III.

CAUTION:

Halāsana keeps the spinal column fully elastic. But people who find their spine stiffened, should start this exercise slowly. No jerks should be given. Jerks may injure the rigid muscles. What little bent is possible should first be secured and maintained for some time. After a while a bigger curve will become possible. In this way, with daily practice, the spine will slowly be restored to its original state of elasticity.

This caution also applies to the practice of Bhujaṅgāsana, Dhanurāsana,

Paśchimatāna and Yoga- Mudrā in particular and to any exercise that involves the bending of the spine in general.

CULTURAL ADVANTAGES:

Halāsana is one of the finest exercises for keeping the spine elastic and the spinal nerves healthy. When we remember that real youth is invariably characterized by an elastic spine and old age always renders the spine rigid, we can at once understand the cultural value of this exercise. Halāsana is also very helpful in developing strong abdominal muscles. In maintaining a healthy thyroid the effect of this Āsana is inferior only to that of Sarvāṅgāsana .

THERAPEUTICAL ADVANTAGES:

Halāsana is useful in combating dyspepsia and constipation, especially when they are due to the degeneration of the abdominal muscles or the nervous mechanism of digestion. The pose is available also for reducing the enlarged liver and spleen, provided that enlargement is not excessive. In particular types of diabetes, this Āsana may be practised with advantage. Also read therapeutical advantages of Bhujaṅgāsana.

FIG 47

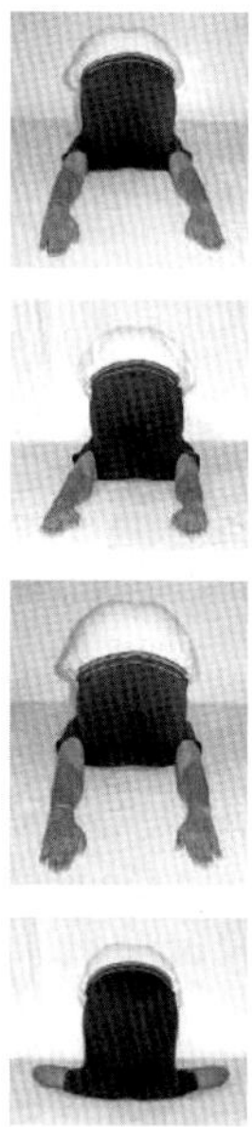

FIG 48

Bhujaṅgāsana or

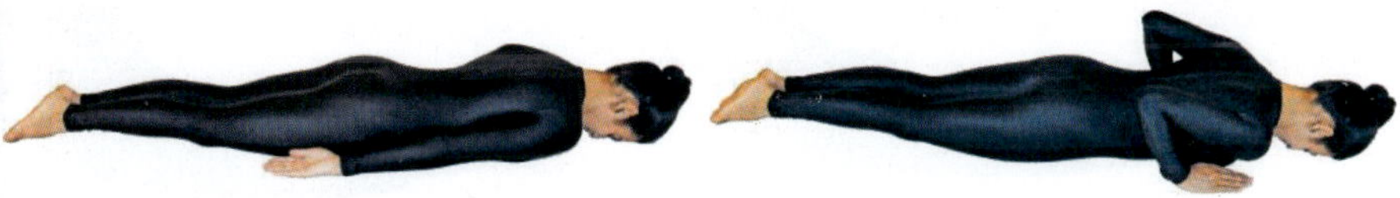

FIG 49

THE NAME:

The pose is called Bhujaṅgāsana because the full display of it gives one the appearance of a hooded snake under irritation with its neck dilated like a hood. (vide Fig. 49). Bhujaṅgāsana means a cobra in Saṅskṛta.

THE TECHNIQUE:

The student first lies prone on his seat with his muscles thoroughly relaxed as shown in Fig. 51. This picture, however, represents the student preparing himself for Śalabhāsana and not for the Cobra Pose which requires a somewhat different arrangement of the hands and forehead. While getting ready for the Cobra Pose the student touches the ground with his forehead; and keeps his hands, one on each side of the chest, bending them in the elbows. The soles are made to look upward.

The student then raises his head and bends the neck backward as far as possible, completely throwing out his chin. During this attempt his chest is kept close to the ground, the trunk, so to say, taking no part in movement. When the head is fully swung backward, the student begins to work the deep muscles of his back. By their contraction he slowly raises his chest. When the student is only a beginner, he supports his rising thorax with his hands, gradually increasing the angle between his arm and forearm. But as he becomes accustomed to this practice, he tries to depend upon the muscles of the back alone for raising his chest; and though the hands are allowed to work

The Cobra Pose

FIG 50

as previously, comparatively little burden is now put upon them. In practising Bhujaṅgāsana the student does not give a full backward curve to his spine all at once; but tries to raise his vertebrae one by one, and marks that the pressure on the spinal curve is travelling down the column step by step, until the thoracic part gets a good backward bend. Here he begins to use his hands more actively; and partly with their help and partly with the help of the deep muscles of the back, starts working the lumbar region. Lastly even the lumbar vertebrae are thrown backward in a curve and the whole pressure is felt at the sacrum. When the Āsana is completed, and the whole spinal column describes a deep curve as seen in Fig. 50. Fig. 49 represents the side view of the full pose. It is to be noted here that the backward bend of the neck has not been shown in the accompanying illustrations, but is not to be neglected in practice.

While the full pose is being maintained the abdominal muscles and especially the two recti are stretched, and the intra-abdominal pressure is greatly increased. If just at this time, an attempt is made to contract these muscles, it largely helps to add to this pressure.

After maintaining the pose for the prescribed time, the student begins to efface the spinal curve and bring down his chest. Here too, he proceeds gradually in his work. First the lumbar curve is obliterated, each vertebra being relieved of its pressure which now travels upwards. The thoracic and cervical curves are effaced in the same way, until the whole spine lies in a horizontal line and the forehead touches the ground as it did originally.

The student, if he is a beginner, does not trifle with his breath, during this exercise. It is allowed to flow as usual. But when he is advanced in his Yogic studies and knows how to control his breath, he may maintain full inspiration throughout the practice.

The exercise may be repeated three to seven times with advantage. In the Full Course the full pose is to be maintained for ten seconds, but in the Short Course it is to be kept up for five seconds only. So far as the Easy Course is concerned, it may be maintained from two to five seconds.

CAUTION:

For caution read Halāsana.

CULTURAL ADVANTAGES:

The deep muscles of the back are alternately contracted and relaxed in working out this pose both ways. The muscles thus exercised gain in health and keep the spine elastic. During their work these muscles secure a liberal blood supply by promoting blood circulation which is ordinarily somewhat slow in this part of the body.

This pose has such a good effect upon the deep muscles, that even a single successful attempt at it, relieves an aching back, if the pain is due to overwork.

The whole spine receives a steady pull anteriorly, every vertebra and its ligaments having their share in the work. If there be any slight displacement in the spinal column, it is adjusted to the normal condition.

All the thirty-one pairs of the spinal nerves exist through spaces left between every two adjoining vertebrae. The two gangliated chains of the sympathetic also stand imbedded in the muscles situated on the two sides of the spinal column. This exercise, by promoting the blood circulation of these parts, very favourably influences these nerves and help them in maintaining their health and activity. Bhujaṅgāsana considerably influences the development of the abdominal muscles.

THERAPEUTICAL ADVANTAGES:

Bhujaṅgāsana along with Śalabhāsana or Ardha-Śalabhāsana and Dhanurāsana may best be practised in combination with Halāsana. The combination accentuates the results expected of the Plough Pose.

People suffering from flatulence immediately after meals, should emphasize Bhujaṅgāsana; but those that feel flatulent some time after the meals, should devote more tome to Śalabhāsana or Ardha-Śalabhāsana. Dhanurāsana may be useful to people of both the types. Unlike Halāsana these three or four Āsanas have no direct influence upon the thyroid.

Śalabhāsana or

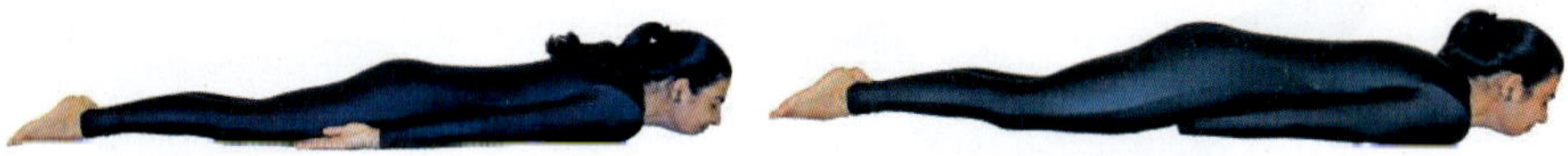

FIG 51

THE NAME:

The pose is called Śalabhāsana because its full show lends one the appearance of a locust with its tail standing at an angle with the ground. (vide Fig 52). Śalabha means a locust in Saṅskṛta.

THE TECHNIQUE:

As illustrated in Fig. 51, the student lies prone on his seat with his soles looking upwards and his fingers clenched. He stretches his hands along his body so that his shoulders and the backs of his fists touch the ground. He either rests his chin, mouth and nose on his seat; or his chin alone, the head being thrown a little backward. Then with a full inspiration he stiffens his whole body; and tries to raise his lower extremities backwards, putting his whole weight on the chest and hands. The wrists especially feel the burden of the lifted legs. Throughout the exercise the breath is held in and the knees are kept stiff and straight. In this practice the sacrum shares the fate of the legs and is a little raised with them.

When the student finds that he can no longer hold in his breath, he slowly lowers down his legs, relaxes his muscles, and gradually proceeds to exhale. When respiration becomes normal, the student is ready for the next attempt.

The pose may be repeated three to seven times with advantages. Care should be taken not to strain the lungs by unduly prolonging the posture.

The Locust Pose

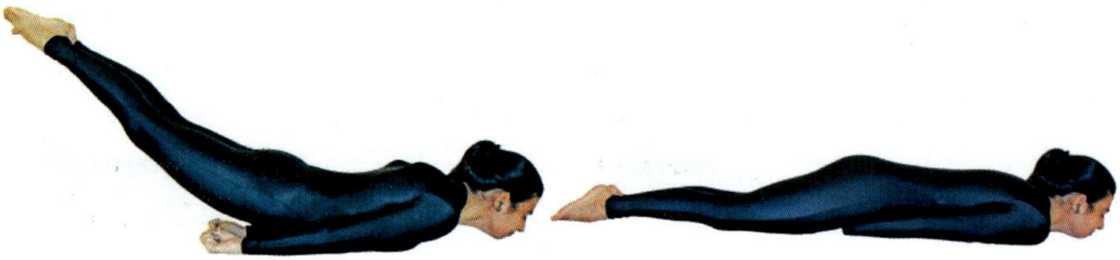

FIG 52

Of all the Āsana, it is only Śalabhāsana which requires a sudden movement of the lower extremities in its practice. But here too no violence should be done to the legs. The action, though sudden, should be perfectly smooth.

It may be readily seen that the trunk and the upper extremities that were put into action during the Cobra Pose, are kept to the seat in this posture; whereas the lower extremities that were passive in the Cobra Pose, are actively used in this exercise.

CULTURAL ADVANTAGES:

Śalabhāsana is a fine exercise for the pelvis and the abdomen.

THERAPEUTICAL ADVANTAGES:

Read what has been said in this regard under Bhujaṅgāsana.

Ardha-Śalabhāsana or The Half Locust Pose

FIG 53

FIG 54

THE NAME:

The name is not taken from any of the original Yogic texts. It is coined by ourselves to express an adaptation of Śalabhāsana, described as follows.

THE TECHNIQUE:

As in the Locust Pose so here the student lies prone on his seat. To begin with all his muscles are kept in a relaxed condition and throughout the exercise breath is allowed to have its normal flow. The practice starts by raising backward one of the legs, of course, after contracting the necessary set of muscles (vide Figs 53 and 54). This raising of one leg the student does so slowly and steadily that little pressure is experienced except on the parts that are actually working. All the while the trunk and the other leg are kept close to the seat. When the leg that is being lifted backward has described the greatest possible angle, it is slowly lowered down to its original position. Then the other leg is raised and taken through the same movement. Thus the two legs go on working alternately till the desired amount of exercise is done. Control of breath and stiffening of muscles may be introduced as the practice advances, care being taken to see that no strain is put upon the system on that account. After one feels strong enough to tackle the full Locust Pose, that should be substituted for the Half Locust Pose.

CULTURAL AND THERAPEUTICAL ADVANTAGES:

Ardha-Salabhāsana gives the same advantage as Śalabhāsana, but only on a humbler scale.

Dhanurāsana or The Bow Pose

FIG 55

THE NAME:

The pose is called Dhanurāsana because in this posture the body resembles a bow with its string attached to it. The trunk and the thighs represent the bow proper, whereas the hands and legs take the place of a string. Dhanus, in Saṅskṛta, means a bow.

THE TECHNIQUE:

As in the last two or three poses, the student lies prone on his seat with his chin resting thereon. He bends his legs in the knee-joint, until they are well folded upon the thighs; and are available to the hands that try to grasp them in the ankles. When the hands get a good hold upon the legs, the student tries to raise his trunk as well as his knees, until his whole body stands on his seat curving upwards both ways. The whole pressure of his body is thrown upon the abdomen, and the extremities are fully stretched as shown in Fig. 55. After maintaining the pose for the desired time, the chest and the knees are lowered to the seat. The hands let go the legs which are straightened out, the hands themselves being made to lie on the two sides of the trunk.

This exercise requires rather a brisk movement of the body. Hence care should be taken not to sprain any joint. The Āsana may be maintained for something like five seconds to begin with. The period being afterwards increased to three minutes or more, according to one's capacity. During the practice breath may be allowed to flow as usual, or it may be controlled, if this could be done without any damage to the lungs. It is desirable for a novice to keep his knees apart because thereby, he would be able to secure a greater curve for his body during this exercise. As the muscles become more and more elastic, the knees should be drawn closer, till at last they should be made to stand together, carrying the intra-abdominal pressure to its highest limit. In Fig. 55 the knees are shown close to each other. Fig. 56 gives the back view of the posture.

CULTURAL ADVANTAGES:

It will be readily seen that this posture is a combination of the two exercises, Bhujaṅgāsana and Śalabhāsana. Naturally it claims the advantages of both, though on a humbler scale. The intra-abdominal pressure here is not as great as in the Locust Pose, because even with full inspiration, the diaphragm does not press upon the abdominal viscera as tightly in this practice as in Śalabhāsana. The deep muscles of the back are exercised much better in Bhujaṅgāsana than in this pose; because there they are mainly responsible for the backward curve of the trunk, whereas in this pose their work is largely done by the hands and legs tugging at each other. Again the wave of contraction and relaxation travelling up and down the spinal column and which forms the principal feature of Bhujaṅgāsana, is missed here. This pose has, however, a special advantage which can not be derived from the two preceding Āsanas that are combined in it. The two recti as well as the other muscles of the abdomen that flex the hip-joints, are more fully stretched in this pose, than in the other two. This is due to raising backward simultaneously both the trunk and the thighs.

THERAPEUTICAL ADVANTAGES:

For therapeutical advantages read what is said in this regard under Bhujaṅgāsana.

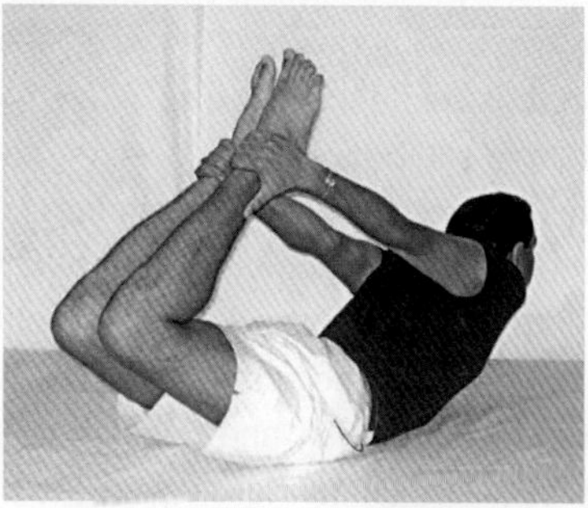

FIG 56

Ardha-Matsyendrāsana or The Half Matsyendra Pose

FIG 57

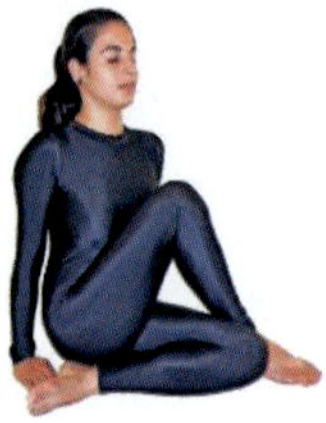

FIG 58

FIG 59

THE NAME:

The pose is called Ardha-Matsyendrāsana because it does not require entire technique of the full Matsyendra Pose. The full posture was invented by Bhagavān Matsyendra, one of the pioneers of Yogic culture. Although of high spiritual value, the original pose is somewhat difficult to practise. Hence it has been omitted from this handbook. The half Matsyendra Pose is easy to practise and has physiological advantages too.

THE TECHNIQUE:

To start with, the student sits on his seat with his legs fully stretched out and placed close to each other. (vide Fig. 38). He then bends in the knee one of his legs, say the right, and folding it upon the thigh, sets its heels tight on the perineum which indicates the region between the anus and scrotum in the male, and between the anus and the vulva in the female. If we feel this part of the body with our fingers, we find two hard bones on the two sides with a soft part between. It is against this soft part that the heel is to be set. Care must be taken not to allow any portion of the scrotum to slip between the heel and the perineum. This can be done by lifting the whole scrotum with the left hand while the right hand is engaged in arranging the right heel. Sometimes an attempt is made to sit on the heel, but this is a wrong procedure and should be studiously avoided. When properly adjusted the right sole will closely touch the left thigh. (vide Fig. 57). Then the student withdraws his left leg and bending it in the knee, arrange it in such a way that the left foot rests on the right side of the right thigh. (vide Fig. 58).

The main feature of the pose consists in twisting the spinal column. The steps taken up to now are only preparation for securing this twist with mechanical advantage derived from particular arrangements of the extremities. The erect knee, here the left, is now to be used as a fulcrum upon which the right shoulder-joint is to rest its back. (vide Figs. 59 and 60). This is done by passing the right hand round the left knee and rotating the whole trunk to the left, until the right shoulder and the left knee stand pressing against each other. With a view to obtain a full rotation of the trunk and to prevent the knee slipping off the shoulder, the right hand is fully stretched out and made to grasp the left foot or its toe which is now available on the wrong side. Care should be taken not to strain the elbow-joint, as such a strain is likely to result in a fracture. The danger is completely avoided by firmly setting the shoulder against the knee.

In order to obtain additional mechanical advantage for securing the spinal twist, the student now employs the left hand. He swings it back and tries to have a hold upon the right thigh just below the groin. Fig. 60 shows the left hand swung back and Fig. 59 represents the fingers clutching the thigh. Thus there are two forces operating upon the two upper corners of the trunk twisting it to the left, and these two together are competent to effect the fullest possible twist. The contrivance, however, does not affect the cervical vertebrae. In order that these might co-operate with the remaining, the head is swung to the extreme left until the chin finds itself almost in a line with the left shoulder. Figs. 59 and 60 represent the full Ardha-Matsyendrāsana, the first picture giving the front and the second giving the back view of the same. Throughout the practice, the student takes care to see that his chest stands erect and does not droop down. The same pose is to be tried using the left extremities instead of the right and vice versa so that the two opposite twists would move between them the different vertebrae through all the rotating space available.

The pose may be practised only for some seconds to start with, the maximum period to be devoted to each side being not more than a minute. For a student of general physical culture one twist each side is sufficient; but for curative purposes these twists may be repeated according to individual strength.

CULTURAL ADVANTAGES:

If the spinal column is to be maintained in the best of health, it must be trained to execute all the movements through which it is capable of going. The natural movements of the spine may be of six varieties; forward and backward bends, side bends to the right and left, the left and the right twist. In doing Sarvāṅgāsana, Halāsana, Paśchimatāna and Yoga-Mudrā we educate the spine in forward bents. The training of backward bents is given to the vertebral column in Matsyāsana, Bhujaṅgāsana, Śalabhāsana and Dhanurāsana. Ardha-Matsyendrāsana in one pose gives the two side twists with the greatest efficacy and as such has a very great cultural value. This pose also secures the side bends for the spine, although not on a large scale. Hence every scheme for the culture of the spine must find a prominent place for Ardha-Matsyendrāsana and must co-ordinate it with the backward and forward movements of the spinal column.

THERAPEUTICAL ADVANTAGES:

As a curative measure Ardha-Matsyendrāsana can be effectively prescribed against constipation and dyspepsia. Against enlarged and congested liver and spleen and inactive kidneys, it could be practised with advantage. In order to reap the highest therapeutical benefit, this pose should be combined with other exercises that may be indicated by the condition of the patient.

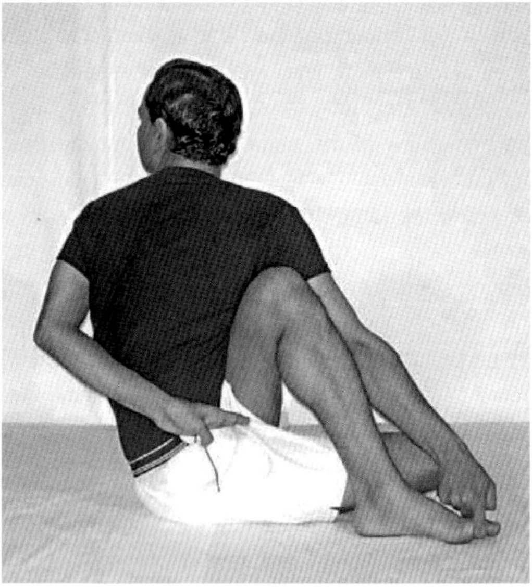

FIG 60

Vakrāsana or

THE NAME:

The pose is called Vakrāsana because in taking it, the spinal column is twisted. In Sanskṛta Vakra means twisted. Vakrāsana is only simplification of Ardha-Matsyendrāsana and has been introduced in Yogic culture by Śrimat Kuvalayānanda as an easier exercise preparatory to that pose.

THE TECHNIQUE:

To begin with the student takes his seat stretching out his legs so as to keep them close together. Then he raises one of his knees, say the right, and withdraws his foot until it rests by the side of his left knee. Next he places his right hand behind his back without much twisting his trunk. Thereafter the left arm is passed round the right knee from outside and the left palm is placed on the ground. In doing this the student pushes the right knee as far to the left as possible, all the while trying to twist his trunk to the right as best as he can. The knee is, however, kept firmly in its position, offering good resistance to the opposite arm. The last part of the technique is gone through when the student turns his face to the right, until his chin finds itself coming exactly over the right shoulder. This secures a complete twist to the right for the spinal column. Fig. 61 illustrates the right spinal twist.

Instead of starting with the right knee the student can start with the left and obtain the left vertebral twist. Fig. 62 illustrates the left spinal twist.

The Twisted Pose

FIG 62

The right and left twists put together should not take more than three minutes as the maximum time devoted to them.

CULTURAL & THERAPEUTICAL ADVANTAGES:

Vakrāsana is Ardha-Matsyendrāsana simplified. As such it claims all the advantages of the latter pose, although they are available in this Asana on a moderate scale.

FIG 61

Siṃhāsana or The Lion Pose

FIG 63

FIG 64

THE NAME:

The pose is called Siṃhāsana because in it the student imitates the lion with his jaws thrown wide apart and his tongue fully stretched out. Siṃha means a lion in Saṅskṛta.

THE TECHNIQUE:

To start with the student fully stretched out his legs on his seat. Then he bends one of his legs, say the right, in the knee, and folds it on the thigh. Now the right foot is to be inserted below the left buttock, so that the student can sit upon the right heel without any discomfort. For this purpose, the sole of the right foot is turned upwards with the hands, and with the left knee raised the right foot is placed under the left buttock, all the while the student resting himself on the right buttock only. When the right foot is satisfactorily arranged below the left buttock the student lifts up the right buttock from the ground, and puts his whole weight upon the right heel. In this position the upturned sole of the right foot will show itself partially from behind the toes will be seen spreading a little beyond the thigh. The sole and the toes as arranged here, can be seen in Fig. 64 which illustrates the back view of the Lion Pose. When the student feels secure on his right heel, he bends his left leg, and anteriorly crossing the right leg from below, sets the foot under the right buttock, so as to enable him to sit on the left heel. The left toes spread out beyond the right thigh. When this is done the student finds himself sitting evenly on both the heels.

In order to secure the necessary ease and comfort which must characterize every Yogic pose, the student hereafter puts his whole weight on the thighs and especially on the knees which are made to rest on the ground. This gives a little forward inclination to the whole trunk, the buttocks being lifted up from behind.

The muscles of the arms and forearms are stiffened, the elbow-joints are fully extended and the palms are made to cover their corresponding knees, the fingers being spread out to imitate the broad paws of the lion.

The trunk along with the spine is held erect, the chest is thrown out, and the braced up shoulders are made to exert a gentle pressure on the knees through the upper extremities.

Then begins the execution of the most important part of Siṃhāsana. The jaws are thrown wide open and the tongue is stretched out to its utmost limit[1] . The eyes are fixed either between the eyebrows as in the Frontal Gaze, or on the tip of the nose as in the Nasal[2] . Siṃhāsana, as it is photographed here, is with the Formal Gaze. Generally, though not necessarily, the chin is pressed against the chest so as to adjust it in the jugular notch in order to form Jālandhara-Bandha[3]. Fig. 63 shows this pose with the Chin-Lock.

Instead of the right leg being taken up first and the left made anteriorly to cross it from below, the left leg may be taken first and the right may be passed underneath it.

During the pose breathing becomes mainly oral, most of the air from the lungs being expelled through the mouth in exhalation and most of the air being drawn into the lungs the same way in inhalation. The nasal passage is very sparingly used for the incoming and outgoing breath.

Yogic physical culturists will do well to take this exercise in the end of their daily programme. Maximum time to be devoted to it should not exceed three minutes.

CULTURAL ADVANTAGES:

The pose by itself has not got much physical value, nor has it got any spiritual

1. This arrangement of the jaws and the tongue constitutes what is known as Siṃha-Mudrā in Yoga.
2. Vide Chapter III
3. Ibid.

value also. So it need not be maintained for any considerable time. A maximum of three minutes has already been prescribed above. Its great physical and therapeutical importance when practised with the Tongue-Lock in rapid succession, has been discussed under Jihvā-Bandha in the next chapter.

It is to be remembered, however, that the Āsana is a very valuable exercise as a preparation for the three Bandhas, Uḍḍiyāna, Mūla and Jālandhra, even when by itself it is not of much consequence either physical or spiritually. The mere widely throwing open of the jaws and the drawing out of the tongue make the muscles of the neck elastic, thus facilitating the formation of the Chin-Lock. The attempt at Jālandhra Bandha, the pressure on the knees exerted through the hands, the bracing up of the spine and the throwing out of the chest, all put together, give a sort of control over the abdominal recti, thus preparing the student for Uḍḍiyāna. Again, lifting up the buttocks with a view to hold the spine erect and sit lightly on the heels, tends to the contraction of such pelvic muscles as facilitate the practise of Mūla Bandha. Thus it will be seen that the Lion Pose is a fine exercise preparatory to the three Bandhas.

THERAPEUTICAL ADVANTAGES:

For these advantages read Jihvā-Bandha in Chapter V.

Vajrāsana or The Pelvic Pose

FIG 65

FIG 66

FIG 67

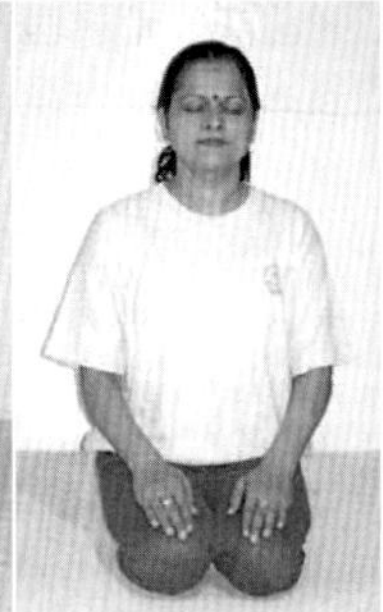

FIG 68

THE NAME:

The pose is called Vajrāsana because it affects the pelvis. The effect of Vajrāsana on the pelvis will be made clearer when the supine variety of this Āsana is studied. (vide Supta Vajrāsana). Vajra in Yogic literature does not mean the pelvis, but it means the penis. So it will be seen that the name Pelvic Pose is only a free rendering of the original name Vajrāsana. It is to be, however, noted that the pose does affect the whole of the pelvis as much as the penis itself.

THE TECHNIQUE:

As in the case of the previous practice, the student fully stretches out his legs on his seat to start with. Then he bends one of his legs, say the left, in the knee and folds it on the thigh. But he does not keep the knee resting on the ground as in the last Āsana, but raises it to its full height while bending it for further action. Thus the foot is made to rest on the ground in front of the left buttock, and the knee stands high up against the left half of the chest. (vide Fig. 65). After this the student raises his left buttock reclining his trunk slightly to the right which is made to rest on the right hand placed by the side of the right thigh. Then with his left hand he catches hold of his left foot, as shown in Fig. 65, and drawing it to the left of the left thigh, gets it fully extended so as to turn the sole upwards. While doing this the knee is lowered to the ground, the toes are arranged behind the slightly raised left buttock, pointing to the right, and the heel is made to lie to the left, clear of the body. Thus the foot and the leg form a sort of a circular curve which is made to surround the left buttock. The right thigh, leg and foot are carried through a similar procedure and are arranged on the right side, the foot again going round the buttock. In this final arrangement of the feet, each heel is kept by the side of the corresponding hip-joint, the upper surface of the feet touch the seat, the soles are turned upwards, and the two sets of the toes lie pointing each other with some space left between them. (vide Fig. 66).

There is another way of arranging the legs and the feet in this pose. Instead of keeping them clear of the thighs and the buttocks, they are placed underneath the latter, so that the student sits on his ankles. Naturally the two sets of toes are not now held apart but they cross on another behind the coccyx. (vide Fig.67).

With the lower extremities thus arranged and with the knees made to lie close together almost touching each other, the student sits erect on his buttocks, holding the spine straight. With the palms covering the knees and the eyes closed in concentration, the technique of the pose is completed.

This Āsana is generally practised for spiritual purposes. When so used its time limit would depend upon the duration of the spiritual exercise.

NOTE:

The name Vajrāsana is often used for Siddhāsana or the Accomplished Pose. When we remember the meaning of the word Vajra in Yogic literature and also take into consideration that in Siddhāsana one of the heels is set at the root of the penis, we can at once understand why the Accomplished Pose is also called Vajrāsana. The significance of the name in the case of the present Āsana has already been explained.

CAUTION:

Those people whose joints are stiff and do not admit of easy movements, should practise this pose with caution. No strain should be allowed. First the joints should be accustomed to be flexed to a greater and greater degree. And when they admit to the necessary bent, the full pose should be attempted.

CULTURAL & THERAPEUTICAL ADVANTAGES:

Vajrāsana is principally a meditative pose. Its physical advantages are not considerable.

Supta-Vajrāsana or The Supine Pelvic Pose

FIG 69

THE NAME:

The pose is called Supta-Vajrāsana because the student lies supine in the Āsana instead of sitting erect as in the original Vajrāsana. In Saṅskṛta Supta means asleep. Fig. 69 illustrates the full pose.

THE TECHNIQUE:

As the practice is only a further development of Vajrāsana, the student arranges his lower extremities as required for practicing the last Āsana. It is needless to say that both the varieties of the Vajrāsana arrangement are available for this development. After the student has assumed Vajrāsana, he tries to lie on his back. This is done step by step. First he reclines backward resting the burden of his trunk upon his hands which are made to serve as props from behind. Then one of the hands is relieved and the burden of the body on that side is thrown upon the elbow which is now made to rest on the seat. The same is done in the case of the other hand. Afterwards even these elbow props are removed and the trunk is made to rest on the shoulder-blades, that is, the large flat bones of the upper part of the back. In the beginning, in this position, the student finds that his spine makes a curve and does not lie in contact with the seat. However, as the practice advances, this curve gradually but considerably effected and the vertebral column is made to lie along the ground as far as possible. Then comes the turn of the upper extremities to be adjusted. For this work the student slightly lifts up his head, because he has to get his arms and forearms to serve as cushions underneath it. One of the hands is then passed below the head and made to grasp the shoulder-joint on the opposite side. The other hand does a similar thing, the two elbows projecting a little beyond the head on the seat. The eyes may be closed to render significant the word Supta occurring in the name of the Āsana.

As Supta-Vajrāsana is a further development of Vajrāsana, the practice of the former should not be started without completely mastering the latter. Special care is to be taken of the ankle-joints which are far more strained in this development than in the original pose. In getting out of the pose, the student first lets go of his hands, then raises his trunk and finally relieves his legs. Any attempt to take off the legs first is likely to injure the ankle-joint. The maximum time to be devoted to this pose should not exceed three minutes for ordinary purposes.

CULTURAL ADVANTAGES:

The abdominal recti are fully stretched and the bowels and other abdominal viscera considerably stimulated, the effects on the pelvic organs being greatly pronounced.

THERAPEUTICAL ADVANTAGES:

Supta-Vajrāsana is a very good remedy for constipation.

Paśchimatāna
or The Posterior Stretching Pose

THE NAME:

The posture is called Paśchimatāna because it stretches the posterior muscles of almost the whole body. In Saṅskṛta Paśchima means the posterior and the root Tān means stretch; and thus Paśchimatāna means stretching the posterior. Textbooks on Yoga give also a spiritual interpretation of the name. The pose is capable of rousing spiritual forces that are felt travelling upward through the spine. It is to connote this capacity of the Āsana that it is called Paśchimatāna.

THE TECHNIQUE:

The student begins by fully stretching out his legs on his seat, and keeping them close to each other (vide Fig. 38). He then bends forward a little, makes hooks of his forefingers, and catches hold of his great toes, the right toe with the right finger and the left with the left. A pull on the great toes with the fingers, secures not only a full relaxation but a complete stretching of the posterior muscles of the legs. The student then further bends forward in the lumbosacral region, and stretching his trunk along his thighs, rests his face on his knees. This entirely doubles his body through the hip-joints. The distance between the shoulders and the toes is much shorter than the hands in this pose. Hence the upper extremities are bent in the elbows, and if possible are made to rest on the ground as shown in Fig. 70. Care is taken not to allow the knees to bend, straight knees being essential for maintaining a full stretch of the lumbosacral region. Fig. 70 gives a side view of the Āsana and Fig. 71 represents a back view of the same.

In the case of nearly every beginner, the hamstring muscles - muscles which when contracted enable us to bend our knee and which are situated at the back of it - do not possess the elasticity necessary for this Āsana. The result is that the knees are raised when one tries to bend over one's thighs. By a little practice, however, young and well-built persons can soon make the hamstring muscles sufficiently supple, so that there is little trouble in securing the desirable bent even without raising the knees.

But people who are advanced in age, or are prematurely old, or have stiffened their muscles by over-exercise stand on a different footing. They experience an amount of difficulty in bending their trunk effectively while maintaining a straight knee.

Their spine is so stiff that they cannot even reach their toes with their fingers. Nay, in some cases their toes remain far beyond the reach of their fingers! However, there is absolutely no reason for these people to become impatient over the matter. They should proceed into the practice of this Āsana slowly and steadily. Instead of trying to catch hold of their great toes, they should seize their legs, either in the ankle or even higher up nearer the knee. Without experiencing much discomfort, the trunk should be bent forward as far as possible, but the knee should always be kept stiff. This little bent maintained for a time, will invariably make further flexing possible. As usual jerks, either violent or mild, should be studiously avoided. In a few days the spine will begin to show signs of improved elasticity and the hamstring muscles will be better able to bear the necessary strain. When the toes are reached they should be hooked by the fingers and the whole system of posterior muscles stretched by degrees. Suppleness will develop day by day ultimately making the full pose not only possible but even comfortable. Patience and perseverance must overcome every difficulty. Regularity is, indeed, essential; but we also advise punctuality. These two will enable almost every Yogic culturist to perform any Āsana within a reasonably short period.

For the purpose of physical culture, not more than three minutes will be the maximum time to be devoted to this pose. As regards the minimum, if a Yogic culturist is able, just in the beginning, to secure the complete bend required for the full Āsana, he may maintain the pose only for fifteen seconds to start with and slowly develop it to one minute only. But if, on account of the stiffness of muscles, only a partial bend becomes possible at the outset, the Yogic culturist should repeat the pose two or three times over and make up to total of one minute. As the spine becomes more and more elastic the three attempts may be fused into one, covering a period of one continuous minute. Three turns of one minute each would make up the maximum of three minutes.

Those who practise the Short Course should maintain the pose for five seconds at a time and should repeat it according to their own measure.

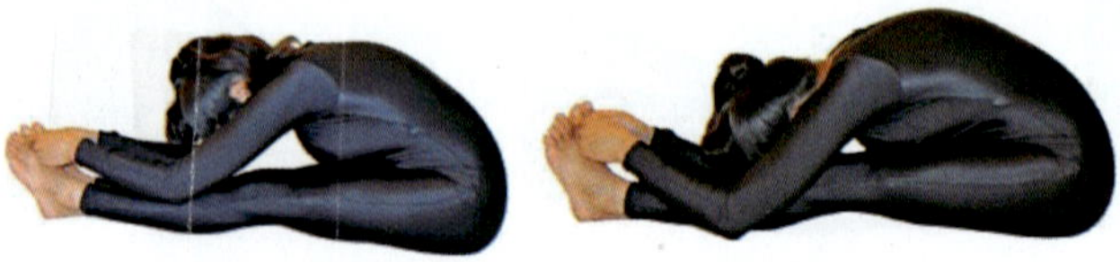

FIG 70

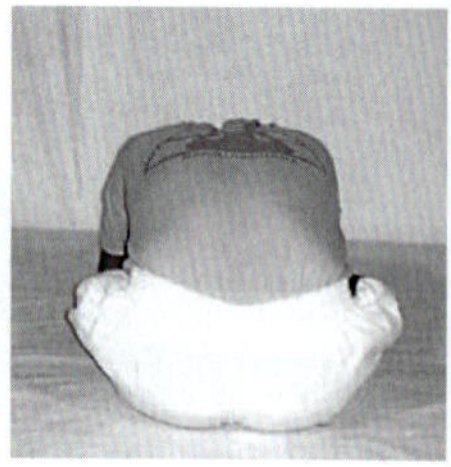

FIG 71

CULTURAL ADVANTAGES:

Paśchimatāna is a fine stretching exercise. Nearly all the posterior muscles of the body and particularly the hamstring muscles at the back of the knees are relaxed and fully stretched. The pose is also of great importance in the culture of the abdomen. The front abdominal muscles are vigorously contracted which ensures better health and functioning for them. Nerves supplying the pelvic organs and arising from the lumbosacral region are toned up because of the exercise of the lumbosacral part of the spine and the consequent richer blood supply brought to this part.

Paśchimatāna is known to have considerable spiritual significance. It has been found to enable a student of spiritual culture to listen to Anāhata Dhvani or the subtle sound. It is also understood to rouse the spiritual force called Kuṇḍalinī. For spiritual purposes, however, the Āsana has to be practised daily for upwards of hour according to the needs and the capacity of the individual practising it.

THERAPEUTICAL ADVANTAGES:

Paśchimatāna builds a powerful abdomen and is found to be a good remedy against constipation and dyspepsia. It may be prescribed with advantages against seminal weakness and also against the possibility of a recurrence of sciatica.

The measures of Paśchimatāna has to be judiciously adjusted. When maintained for a long time, it promotes constipation instead of relieving it. So if the Āsana must be practised across a good length of time either for physical or spiritual advantages, it should always be accompanied by Uḍḍiyāna which can be repeated several times while Paśchimatāna is being maintained. Habitually constipated people should avoid practising Paśchimatāna for anything more than three minutes a day.

Mayūrāsana or

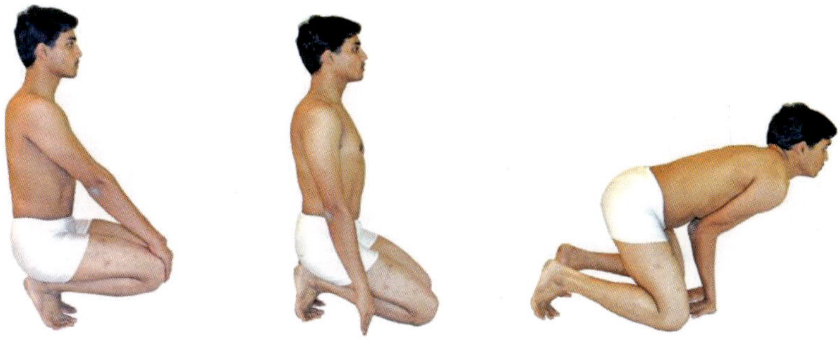

FIG 72

THE NAME:

The pose is called Mayūrāsana because it imitates the deportment of a peacock with his heavy plumage stretching behind him. Mayūra means a peacock in Saṅskṛta.

THE TECHNIQUE:

To start with the student kneels on his seat and brings together his forearms down up to the wrists. The elbow-joints are put in close contact with each other, so that they provide a suitable fulcrum to support the horizontal body, during the full display of the pose. The palms and fingers are made to take the place of the feet and the claws of the peacock. The position of the claws, however, is reversed, the palms being given a backward direction. (vide Fig. 72). It is needless to say that the fingers, when thus arranged, afford a very good contrivance for adjusting the balance of the whole body. (vide Fig. 73).

On the fulcrum thus prepared the body is stretched out in a straight line parallel to the seat. The elbows are placed on the abdomen just below the umbilicus. The forearms do not stand exactly at right angles to the ground, but are a little inclined to the front. The head is raised and the chin thrown out in order to counterbalance the heavy legs. The whole body is held like a horizontal bar resting on a fulcrum. (vide Fig. 73).

A beginner should hold his breath so long as the pose lasts. Quite an amount of muscular energy is required for this exercise, especially in the beginning;

The Peacock Pose

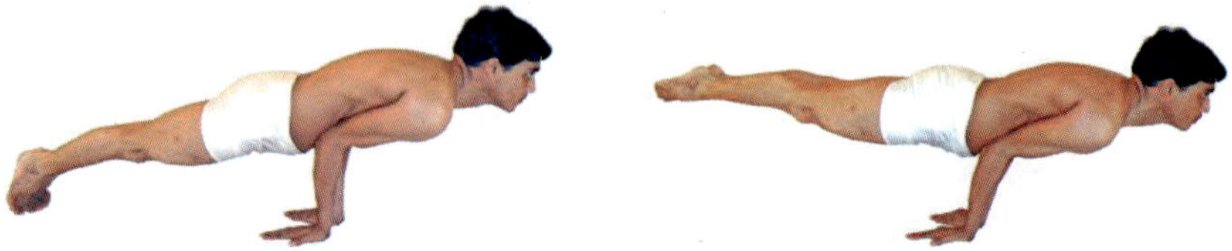

FIG 73

and this energy can best be had with controlled breath. But as the practice advances and the muscles get into the habit of doing this type of work, less energy is needed; and then the breath maintained.

Mayūrāsana is taken advantages of in ejecting the small quantities of water that may be lingering in the colon after practising Basti - Yogic bowel wash. In this connection, however, the pose requires a change in its technique. The legs, instead of being held together and parallel to the ground, are be spread out and raised imitating a proud display of the peacock's plumage.

The change is a physiological necessity. Parallel and horizontal legs require the anal sphincters to be fully contracted. This is quite desirable when the pose is to be practised for itself, because it helps to increase the intra-abdominal pressure which is one of the advantages sought in Mayūrāsana. But when the exercise is done as a sequel to colon flushing, its aim is to drive out the lingering liquid from the large bowel. This requires the anal sphincters to be in a relaxed condition. In order to make this relaxation possible the legs must be spread out. It is to be remembered that the muscles of the buttock remain contracted even in this condition. This contraction, however, does not prevent the ejection of the colon liquid, if the anal sphincters are completely relaxed. The partial contraction of the muscles of the buttocks with a simultaneous relaxation of the anal sphincters, requires some practice in muscle control. In traditional Yogic schools the students are not allowed to practise Basti unless they master this essential technique.

CULTURAL ADVANTAGES:

Mayūrāsana partially checks the flow of the abdominal aorta and thus diverts a liberal blood supply to the digestive organs, rendering them more healthy. These organs are further toned up by the increase in the intra-abdominal pressure which Mayūrāsana causes in its practice.

THERAPEUTICAL ADVANTAGES:

Mayūrāsana is a very good measure against ptosis of the abdominal organs and against dyspepsia. Its usefulness, however, is limited, because in advanced cases of dyspepsia the patient becomes too weak to undergo the strain which this Āsana necessarily involves.

Śavāsana or The Dead Pose

THE NAME:

The pose is called Śavāsana, because it requires complete relaxation of the muscles as in the case of a dead person, whose position the Yogic student is made to imitate in the practice of this posture. Śava means a dead body in Saṅskṛta.

THE TECHNIQUE:

The technique of Śavāsana is simple to understand, but somewhat difficult to practice. It is as follows. The student is to lie on his back, as shown in Fig 74; and fully relax his muscles. It is to be noted here that our muscles remain slightly contracted even when we lie down for rest in a waking condition. Even this slight contraction is to be avoided in the Dead Pose. This requires an effort of will and concentration a little. The student should take a particular part of the body and thoroughly relax its muscles. Then he should concentrate upon that part and imagine that every muscle tissue in that part is further relaxing and is, as it were, collapsing. Constant practice of this procedure will enable the student to bring about full relaxation of different muscles.

Ordinarily he should start with relaxing the thorax. The abdomen should be taken up next. The lower and upper extremities should follow the abdomen, and the brain should come up last. This sequence need not necessarily be followed. However, every student should make his own choice. Many people find it easier to start with the extremities. They take up the trunk later on and finish with the brain. The eyes are to be kept closed. Those who can concentrate themselves even without shutting their eyes, although this is an extremely difficult job, may keep them open, however.

While trying to relax the different parts of his body, the student should attempt relaxation of more than one part conjointly, so that he can ultimately succeed in relaxing all the parts of his body at one and the same time. Complete relaxation of the whole frame is the final aim of Śavāsana.

When the student succeeds in simultaneously relaxing every tissue of his body, he should continue concentrating upon the relaxed tissues for some time. This completes the first part of the technique of Śavāsana.

In the second part while maintaining the bodily relaxation already secured, exclusive attention is to be paid to the regulation of breath. Śavāsana aims at introducing rhythm in the flow of breath. This rhythm can best be introduced through the following stages.

First Stage: - This stage consists in observing one's breath as it flows in and flows out. No attempt is to be made to control it either in volume or in the length of time. Breathing should be allowed to have its own way. This practice of observation is to be slowly developed. To begin with only two or three minutes may be given to it. Afterwards the time should increase to ten minutes. During this as well as during the next two stages, the mind will always have a tendency to wander. This tendency is not only to be checked, but is to be completely overcome. Wholehearted perseverance in practice across a good length of time is the only path that surely leads to success in concentration.

Second Stage: - In about a fortnight's time, the student will find that the breath as it ordinarily flows, is irregular. Not only the inhalation and exhalation are unequal, but each is not very uniform in itself. This uneven and irregular breathing is often responsible for ill-health and needs improvement. So the outgoing and incoming breath should be made to occupy the same length of time. This is best done by lengthening the shorter and shortening the longer one. No effort should be made to increase the volume of each respiration, however. A rhythmical flow is all that is wanted at this stage. The second stage may be practised for nearly quarter of an hour every day. In the beginning a sense of suffocation may be experienced but it will soon disappear.

Third Stage: - In a month or so the student will feel very comfortable at the rhythmical breathing. He should then try to increase the volume of his inhalation

FIG 74

and exhalation by drawing slightly deeper breaths and letting off air proportionately. No violence is to be practised. Breathing is to be as smooth and slow as before, only the breaths are to be very slightly deeper. All the while the mind is to be concentrated upon the moving breath.

The practice of rhythmical breathing is not as easy as it looks to be at the first sight. The most difficult part of it is concentration. Patient work, however, must enable a student to achieve success. There should be no hurry in going through the successive stages. The second stage should not be begun unless and until one has mastered the first. The same is true about the third and second stages.

Rhythmical breathing should be developed very cautiously. At least in the beginning it involves an amount of mental strain. Under no circumstances is this strain desirable. Everything should be comfortable and pleasing. Even after some practice, not more than ten minutes at a time are allowed for patients with weak nerves, although healthy persons may devote as much time to it as they please. The practice may be repeated twice or even thrice a day.

A physical culturist can satisfy himself with the first part of Śavāsana, that is, with the relaxation of his muscles. He need not go in the rhythmical breathing necessarily, although even to him this second part of the Dead Pose will be of great value in improving his nerves. For a spiritual culturist the second part is of utmost importance. It prepares him for his Prāṇāyamic exercises which come after Āsana.

Śavāsana if rightly done is so soothing to the nerves that there is always a tendency to fall asleep during its practice. This tendency is to be checked very studiously, especially by a spiritual culturist who should never get into the habit of lapsing into sleep while he is concentrating his mind.

CULTURAL ADVANTAGES:

(i) Muscles work more efficiently because of their relaxation.
(ii) Venous blood circulation is promoted throughout the body and thus fatigue is relieved.
(iii) The whole nervous system is toned up and mental energy is considerably increased.

THERAPEUTICAL ADVANTAGES:

(i) Śavāsana is helpful in reducing high blood pressure.
(ii) It can effectively overcome neurasthenia.

5

FOUR ADDITONAL EXERCISES

Yoga-Mudrā
Jihvā-Bandha
Viparīta Karaṇī
Nauli

Yoga-Mudrā or

FIG 75

THE NAME:

The compound Yoga-Mudrā is formed of two members: Yoga and Mudrā. In all probability the word Mudrā is used here to mean a symbol; and the exercise is called Yoga Mudrā, because it is useful in awakening the Kuṇḍalinī.

THE TECHNIQUE:

The first step in this practice is to prepare the foot-lock. A reference to Matsyāsana will give detailed information about forming this foot-lock; and Fig. 39 will illustrate the variety of it needs for the practice of Yoga-Mudrā. In this connection it is to be noted that the two heels must press against the portions of the abdomen that they touch. In Fig. 75 the right heel should have been adjusted a little higher up, so that it could have exerted pressure upon the pelvic loop. The left heel is in its place and presses the cecum. After the feet are folded in a lock, the hands are to be folded on the back. This is done by grasping the left wrist in the right hand, as shown in Fig. 76. Next the student bends himself forward and tries to lie that upon his heels, so as to touch the ground with his forehead. Fig. 76 gives the final position.

Care must be taken not to give jerks to the spinal column. Many people find it difficult to secure the necessary bent. They should try to bend as far as they can do so smoothly and comfortably. What little bend may become possible should be maintained for a time. That will enable the student to bend himself further; and after a practice of some days, he will find even the last position quite easy.

The Symbol of Yoga

FIG 76

When Yoga-Mudrā is to be practised as a replacing[1] exercise, the technique requires a little change. The hands instead of being folded upon the back, are to be placed on the heels, so as to grasp them in their hollow. Thus a sort of big ball is available in front of the abdomen, the lowest parts of which are already in contact with it. When the student begins to bend, these parts are pressed, and as he continues to bend still further, the upper parts of the abdomen are also successively pressed in by the convex surface of the rounded hands. In this way a steady upwards pressure is maintained on the abdomen, so that the prolapsed organs are pushed upwards and held in their proper places.

During both these varieties breath is allowed to flow as usual. Exhalation as one bends, is likely to be helpful, especially in the second variety.

When practised as a pelvic exercise, or as a replacing exercise for the whole abdomen, Yoga-Mudrā should last only for few a second - from five to ten at the most. It may be profitably repeated from three to five times at a sitting. For the purpose of the Short or Easy Course five turns in Yoga-Mudrā are sufficient.

When practised as an exercise in nerve culture on the physical side, Yoga-Mudrā may be maintained for three minutes. A spiritual culturist needs a far more liberal measure of this exercise.

---

1. The stomach, the bowels, so also the other abdominal viscera have a tendency to be displaced downwards whenever the muscular wall of the abdomen becomes weak. Nearly every man suffering from chronic constipation also suffers from the displacement of the abdominal organs. Exercises calculated to restore these organs to their original position are called replacing exercises.

CULTURAL ADVANTAGES:

Yoga-Mudrā builds a powerful abdominal wall, helps the abdominal organs to be kept in their proper places, and tones up the nervous system in general and the lumbosacral nerves in particular. Spiritually its prolonged practice helps to rouse the Kuṇḍalinī.

THERAPEUTICAL ADVANTAGES :

The cecum and the pelvic loop are usual seats of bad constipation. In this practice the left heel presses against the cecum and the right against the pelvic loop. This pressure when slowly, steadily and repeatedly applied, has power to stimulate these parts to action; and thus to reduce constipation. Yoga-Mudrā relieves constipation also replacing the displaced abdominal viscera.

Yoga-Mudrā has also been found useful in overcoming seminal weakness.

Jihvā-Bandha or The Tongue-Lock

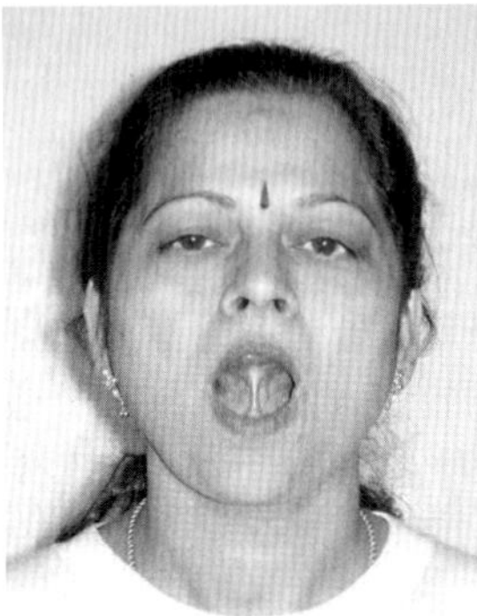

FIG 77

This Bandha is secured by tightly pressing the upper surface of the tongue against the hard and soft palates forming the roof of the mouth, the borders of the tongue being accommodates inside the encircling teeth of the upper jaw. The middle line of the tongue is composed of tough, fibrous tissues and can exert an upward pressure upon the palates more effectively than the side muscles. The tightened tongue covers the whole of the hard palate and as much of the soft palate as lies between the hard palate and the line joining the farthest teeth on the two sides. Those parts of the tongue that lie beyond this line and descend into the throat, experience an upward pull brought on by the stiffened and uplifted tongue. In Saṅskṛta Jihvā means the tongue and Bandha means a lock. Fig 77. illustrates the position assumed by the tongue in the practice.

The Tongue-Lock can be prastised independently or as a part of Viparīta Karaṇī which appears as the next exercise in this chapter. In both these cases the mouth is kept shut. There is one occasion, however, when this lock is required to be done with open mouth. This is when Jihvā-Bandha is being practised as a preliminary to Khecarī. A prominent feature of this Khecarī Mudrā consists of hiding and raising the tongue behind the soft palate. These movements of the tongue are checked by the frenum, which ties that organ to the floor below. (vide Fig. 77). Hence this tie is required to be cut. The traditional position to be given to the tongue when frenum is to be cut for Khecarī, is obtained by doing Jihvā-Bandha.

Jihvā-Bandha can be made to alternate with great advantage with Siṃha-Mudrā [1].

1. Vide page 100, foot note 1.

When so practised the movements of the tongue should be rapid, although the fastening of the tongue and letting it out should be done securely and thoroughly.

Jihvā-Bandha should be practised with an open mouth, when it is made to alternate with Siṃha-Mudrā.

For the purposes of physical culture Jihvā-Bandha alternating with Siṃha-Mudrā may be practised independent of any Āsana or even while sitting in Siṃhāsana.

N.B. - The cultural and therapeutical advantages to be presently mentioned, can best be obtained from Jihvā-Bandha when it is made to alternate with Siṃha-Mudrā.

CULTURAL ADVANTAGES:

(i) Muscles of the neck are exercised and the blood circulation therein is improved.
(ii) Cervical nerves and ganglis are rendered healthier.
(iii) The pharynx and the larynx are exercised and their health is promoted.
(iv) The thyroid is rendered healthier.
(v) The auditory apparatus is made more efficient.
(vi) The salivary glands function more satisfactorily.

THERAPEUTICAL ADVANTAGES:

(i) Congestion in the pharynx is removed.
(ii) Tonsillitis of certain types is checked.
(iii) Deafness due to the thickening of the drum of the ear is relieved.

Viparīta Karaṇī or The Inverted Action

THE NAME:

The exercise is called Viparīta Karaṇī, because in this practice, the whole body is inverted or is made to stand upside-down. In Saṅskṛta Viparīta means inverted and Karaṇī means an action. Textbooks on Yoga give an interpretation of this practice which we have not yet succeeded in exactly interpreting in terms of modern anatomy and physiology. When we do that, we shall be able to give a better explanation of the name by which this practice goes.

THE TECHNIQUE:

The student first lies supine on his seat with all his muscles completely relaxed as shown in Fig. 33. Then he slowly raises his legs through the hip-joint until they make an angle of 30 degrees with the ground. Here the legs are kept steady for a few seconds, and then raised through another 30 degrees. Again they are kept steady here and again raised so as to complete a right angle. This is maintained for a few seconds[1].

Up to now the student does not bring into action his arms and elbows which play only a passive part. But now in his subsequent movements, he has to use his arms and elbows somewhat actively. After keeping his legs in a perpendicular position for a few seconds, the student raises his hips and curves up the trunk, keeping his legs in the same erect position, that they have already assumed. The weight of the body thus raised, is supported by stiffening the arms that are still stretching along the ground. Here the trunk does not make a right angle with the ground as in Sarvāṅgāsana, but simply takes an upward curve. Then the forearms are bent through the elbows and the hands are made to support the curving frame at the hip-bones, as shown in Fig. 79. The posterior part of the head, of the neck, of the shoulder-blades, and of the arms up to the elbows are made to lie along the ground, as seen in Fig. 78, which gives a side view of Viparīta Karaṇī. The chest does not press against the chin as in Sarvāṅgāsana, but keeps itself away from the chin.

---

1. Vide page 76, foot note 1.

The eyes are either closed to concentrate the mind upon a particular part in the body or are kept fixed upon the toes. Then the student forms the Tongue-Lock as already explained (see last exercise), and thus completes the Inverted Action. Fig. 78 illustrates the exercise as seen from the right side of the student.

According to the Yogic texts, the practice begins with twenty-four seconds on the first day, adding a few seconds every day to the period. The maximum stated is three hours. For an exclusive practice of Viparīta Karaṇī in the case of a man of average health, we would recommend twenty-four minutes as the maximum. But if this Inverted Action is to be gone through along with other exercises, we would reduce the maximum to six minutes only.

NOTE:

The points of difference between the technique of Viparīta Karaṇī and that of Sarvāṅgāsana should be carefully noted and observed in practice.

CULTURAL & THERAPEUTICAL ADVANTAGES:

In Hatha-Yoga the Inverted Action is looked upon as the most important practice capable of developing supreme vitality. It is said to be so wonderfully effective that it would rejuvenate an old body in six months. We do not propose any examination of these claims here. One thing is certain the practice combines, though on a humbler scale, all the advantages of

FIG 78

Śīrṣāsana and Sarvāṅgāsana, and as such must have great influence upon the vital forces in the body. All the cautions, however, that are given to the students of Sarvāṅgāsana, are also to be given to the students of this practice.

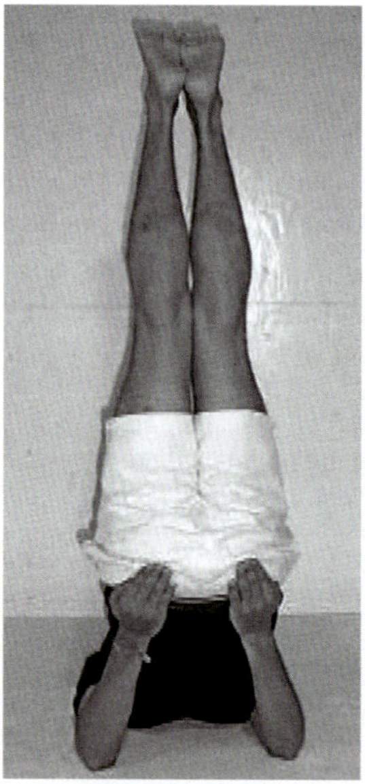

FIG 79

Nauli or The Isolation and Rolling

FIG 80

Nauli is an abdominal exercise. Its principal feature is the isolation and rolling manipulation of the abdominal recti. Generally it is practised in standing, although its practice in a squatting position is required at the timc of Dasti - Yogic flushing of the colon.

The way to Nauli lies through Uḍḍiyāna. In fact Nauli may be equated to Uḍḍiyāna plus the isolation and rolling manipulation of the recti. What it means is this. While practising Nauli the student has to go through the whole technique of Uḍḍiyāna: and then while maintaining Uḍḍiyāna, has to isolate the abdominal recti and roll them from right to left and from left to right, clockwise and counter-clockwise.

For securing Uḍḍiyāna, as we have already seen, the student has first to fix up his neck and shoulders and then to try mock inhalation preceded by the deepest possible expiration. Simultaneously with this he has to relax completely all the muscles that go to form the front portion of the abdominal wall. For practising Nauli the position thus secured is to be treated as a preparatory position.

While maintaining Uḍḍiyāna the student repeatedly gives a forward and downward push to the abdominal point just above the pubic bones. This is the point where the two recti originate. A push at this point brings about contraction of these muscles while it leaves the other muscles of the front abdominal wall in a relaxed condition. Some idea of the nature of this push can be had by imitating the straining of the constipated people when going to stool. The difference in that straining and this push, however, is as follows. In straining the whole pressure is

Manipulation of The Abdominal Recti

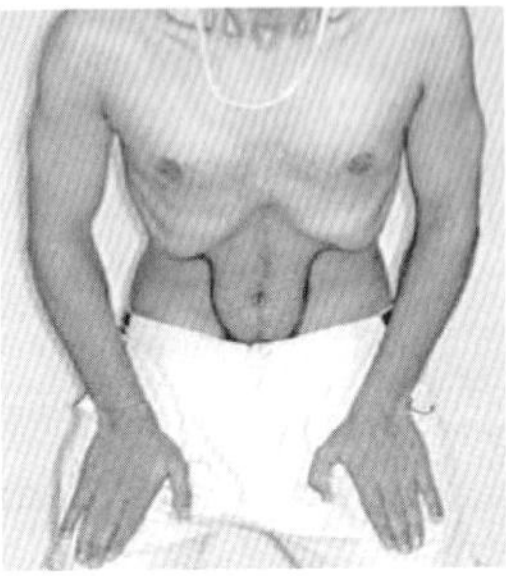

FIG 80

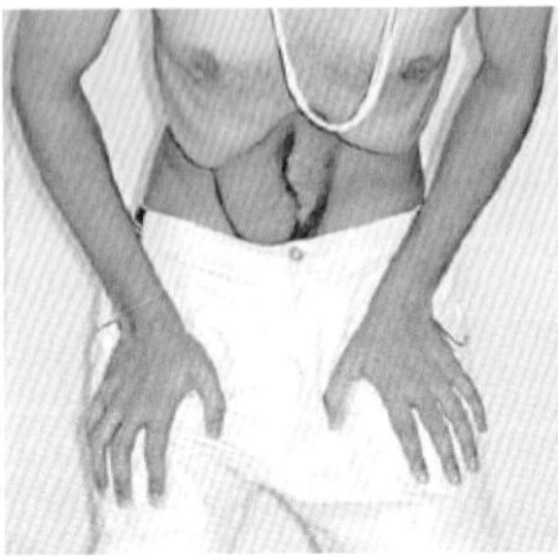

FIG 81

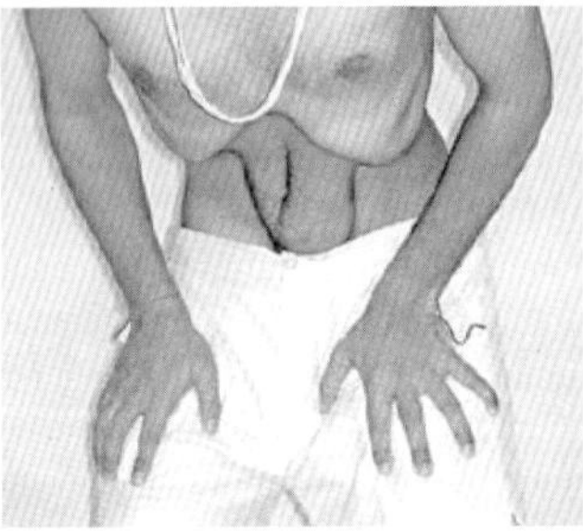

FIG 82

exerted downward whereas in this push it is exerted forward as well as downward. Again in straining, all the abdominal muscles are brought into play, whereas in attempting Nauli, only those muscles which originate from the pubic bones. Repeated attempts at pushing out at the point above the pubic bones, will isolate the recti from the adjoining muscles, because the muscles will be kept in a relaxed condition, whereas, the recti will be contracted. In every case of muscular isolation, the isolated muscle is contracted while the neighboring muscles stand relaxed and inactive.

Once the two recti are isolated at the origin, their isolation will be almost automatically completed right up to the points where they are attached to the ribs above. When the process of isolation is thus completed, the recti will stand side by side vertically crossing the abdomen as shown in Fig. 80. This is called Nauli-Madhyama or the Central Aspect of Nauli.

Very often people fail to hit the exact point against which the pushing business is to proceed. In that case the whole abdomen is pushed out, the recti and other muscles as well. Nor is there any contraction secured. This error is to be studiously avoided. The whole attention is to be concentrated on the point just above the pubic bones. As soon as the student sees that he has not hit the right point, the push should be abandoned there and then, and a fresh attempt should be made in the right direction. Patience is sure to achieve success.

Nauli-Madhyama is only the first part of the whole exercise of Nauli. But there should be no hurry to proceed to the next part of it, unless and until full mastery over this part is obtained. The following tests may be applied to see whether real mastery over Nauli-Madhyama has been secured. The isolation must be complete. The isolation may be known to be thorough, only when thin contracted recti stand out very prominently, projecting themselves from the remaining part of the abdomen that comparatively sinks very deep under the ribs. (ii) The isolation must be easy. That is, there should be absolutely no labour required to bring out the recti, nor to withdraw them. Their projection and retraction must become possible several times in the same exhalation with the greatest facility. (iii) The isolation must be painless. Some thin people who happen to have cultivated good muscles in their youth, can stand the first two tests in practising Nauli-Madhyama; but because of some intestinal disorders find the practice painful. Such persons should not try Nauli at all, till they get rid of the pain by some other means.

We particularly insist upon one's mastering Nauli-Madhyama because upon it mainly depends the efficiency one would get in the practice of Nauli as a whole. Not only this, but the success in Basti and Vajrolī also directly depends upon one's control over Nauli-Madhyama.

The next step in the practice of Nauli is to keep contracted and isolated the right and the left rectus alternately, while the left and right rectus along with the neighboring muscles stand relaxed. When the right rectus alone is contracted and rolled off to the extreme right, it is called Dakshina Nauli. Again when the left rectus alone is contracted and rolled off to the extreme left, is called Vāma Nauli. Figs. 81 and 82 illustrate Dakshina and Vāma Nauli respectively[1].

We shall now proceed to see how this is done. While maintaining Nauli-Madhyama the student bends forward evenly over his thighs. Now if he wants to practise Dakshina Nauli, he bends forward still further on the right hand side, but stand a little erect on the left side. So also he gives his whole trunk a little lateral bent to the right. This sideward forward bending makes the right rectus still more contracted and pushes it to the right side of the abdomen. Simultaneously the straightening of the left side allows the left rectus to be relaxed, of course this relaxation being about by a conscious effort of the will.

---

1. It may be noted that the practice of this exercise requires the head to hang down, so that the student can observe his abdominal work and concentrate upon the contracting muscles.

If the student wants to practice Vāma Nauli, after securing Nauli-Madhyama, he bends forward still further on the left and also gives a lateral bent to his trunk on that side. Side by side the right half of the trunk is held a little more erect. An effort is made to relax the right rectus. These operations will succeed in keeping the left rectus contracted and getting it rolled off to the left of the abdomen.

When the student gets full control of these three aspects of Nauli, he becomes ready for the final operations of rolling the recti clockwise and counter-clockwise several times over without a break in motion. These rolling manipulations alone go by the name of Nauli strictly speaking.

This performance depends upon a very cordial co-operation between the two recti. The two muscles are made to maintain a vertical wave across the abdomen that travels from left to right and from right to left so quickly that it becomes impossible even for an expert eye to follow its progress from point to point. Let us see how this is done.

Starting from Nauli-Madhyama, the left rectus is rolled off to the extreme left and the right rectus is kept relaxed. When the left rectus reaches the extreme left, it is relaxed there and then and simultaneously the right rectus is projected on the extreme right of the abdomen. From there it is rolled to the middle where it begins to disappear (because it is relaxed), and its place is taken by the fully contracted left rectus which carries on the wave of contraction to the extreme left, thus completing one round of Nauli. Several such rounds are taken in one exhalation. All the manipulations of the recti done in one exhalation constitute what we in our literature call one turn.

Similar wave of contraction can be made to travel from left to right also.

The maximum number of turns an average man of health can take in his daily practice of Nauli is seven. There is no harm if a strong man takes even as many as twenty-one of the exercise every-day.

Nauli is strictly to be practised with an empty stomach.

LIMITATIONS:

- People above forty should not attempt this exercise unless they are advised by an expert.

- People suspected of T. B. of the abdomen should never attempt Nauli on their own responsibility.
- Sufferers from chronic appendicitis should avoid this exercise, if it is not recommended by an expert.
- People suffering from high blood pressure should never take to Nauli.
- The exercise is not available to boys and girls before the age of puberty.

CULTURAL ADVANTAGES:

Best exercise for preserving and promoting the health of all the abdominal viscera.

THERAPEUTICAL ADVANTAGES:

(i) An excellent remedy against dyspepsia and constipation.
(ii) Can correct faulty liver, spleen, pancreas and the kidneys.
(iii) Can overcome ovarian insufficiency.
(iv) Can stop painful menstruation under particular circumstances.

6

SCIENTIFIC SURVEY[1] of YOGIC POSES

As stated in the second chapter, Āsanas forms the third item of the Yogic curriculum. These Āsanas can be divided into two groups, namely, meditative and cultural. The aim of the cultural poses is to produce physiological balance in the different systems working in the human body, so that it can possess the best organic vigour. They are specially intended to take particular care of the spinal column, and through it and also through other parts of the body to train the spinal cord and the brain, so that both of them can sustain the interaction of the spiritual force of Kuṇḍalinī when the same is awakened with advanced Yogic practices. These cultural Āsanas involve different physical movements before the final pose is assumed, and the final arrangement of the various parts of the body, being essentially of an out-of-the-way fashion, renders meditation difficult, if not impossible.

1. This survey of the field of Āsanas is by no means complete. We have mapped out only the most important landmarks. For exhaustive information of some of the points touched in this chapter we refer our readers to our article on the rationale of Yogic poses in Yoga Mīmāṁsā, Vols. II and III.

Śīrṣāsana, Sarvāṅgāsana, Halāsana and others treated in the fourth chapter fall under this category. The aim of the meditative poses is to offer a comfortable posture for Prāṇāyāma, Pratyāhāra, Dhāraṇā etc. and in co-ordination with other Yogic exercises to help the student of Yoga in the awakening of Kuṇḍalinī. These meditative poses are such as can be maintained for hours without much discomfort. They do not involve in their technique any out-of-the-way movements of the body, and are in their final stage some variety of ordinary sitting, with a few changes introduced to make the pose more useful for the purpose of meditation. In the third chapter, we have studied four meditative poses - Padma, Siddha, Svastika and Sama. In the present chapter we wish to pass under rapid survey all the Āsanas[2] described in this handbook and try to see whether there is any scientific justification for claiming for them the results that they are declared to bring about. We shall first take up the cultural poses.

As stated in the foregoing paragraph cultural poses are claimed to produce two results -

(i) Giving best organic vigour to the whole body.

(ii) Training the spinal cord and the brain for the interaction of Kuṇḍalinī.

Let us proceed to examine the first claim. As can be seen from the first chapter, all organs of the human body are made up of tissues. If these tissues could be kept in perfect health the human body becomes capable of showing the best organic vigour. Now if we study the conditions necessary for maintaining the health of the different tissues of the human body and if we find that the cultural poses are capable of bringing about these conditions, we can come to the conclusion that these poses can claim to yield the best organic vigour. Let us, therefore, briefly study the conditions which ensure the health of the tissues.

According to the science of physiology, three conditions may be considered to be of vital importance for maintaining the health of the tissues, namely, (i) constant supply of proper nourishment and of the internal secretions of the endocrine glands, (ii) effective removal of waste products, and (iii) healthy functioning of the nerve-connections. Now the elements of nourishment required

2. In this survey we are going to take into account the four additional exercises described in the fifth chapter, although these exercises cannot be called Āsanas technically. In fact the present chapter is a scientific study of all the practices contained in the Full Course (vide appendix I) except the three breathing exercises of Ujjāyī, Kapālabhāti and Bhastrikā, which have already been scientifically evaluated in our handbook Prāṇāyāma.

by the tissues consist of proteins, fats, sugars, salts and oxygen. They are all carried to the tissues by the blood. The first four elements are derived from the food and drink a man takes; and their supply is dependent not only upon the quantity and quality of food and drink taken by the man, but also upon the power of digestion and absorption of his digestive system. So we see that the digestive and the circulatory systems must be kept in an efficient condition, if the tissues are to be fed properly with proteins, fats, sugar and salts. We have, therefore, first to examine the efficacy of Āsana in maintaining the efficiency of these two systems.

Taking the digestive system into consideration first, we find that the principal organs responsible for digestion are the stomach, the small intestine, the pancreas and the liver. All of them are situated in the abdominal cavity which is supported by the pelvis from below and by very strong muscles on all the other sides. Nature has made ample provision for maintaining the health of the digestive organs by arranging for an automatic and gentle massage of these organs for all the twenty-four hours of the day. To understand how this massage is carried out, one has to observe the abdominal movements of a man in normal respiration. With every exhalation the front abdominal muscles are contracted and they push all the abdominal viscera including the organs of digestion inwards and upwards. In doing this they gently massage these abdominal viscera. Again at the time of inhalation the diaphragm presses the abdominal viscera downward and forward; and the relaxing abdominal muscles while being driven forward by the pressing viscera, again give them a gentle massage. In this way something like fourteen to eighteen times every minute the digestive organs are being massaged by the abdominal muscles gently and automatically. This gentle and automatic massage is the most important provision made by nature for keeping the digestive organs healthy. Now it is obvious that this automatic massage can be effectively given only if the abdominal muscles are strong and elastic. But if they are weak, they cannot massage the abdominal organs properly, and indigestion is the result. In people suffering from dyspepsia, these abdominal muscles are found to be too rigid or too weak. Hence, if perfect digestion is to be secured, the abdominal muscles must be kept strong and elastic. Do the Yogic poses make any provision for preserving the strength and elasticity of the abdominal muscles? Yes, they do. The Yogic poses not only keep the abdominal muscles strong and elastic, thus ensuring an effective automatic massage of the digestive organs, but they also make a special provision for giving a forced and vigorous internal massage to the abdominal organs with such a degree of efficiency as is hardly to be met with in any other system of health culture.

It is an admitted scientific fact that muscles can maintain their strength and elasticity, if they are subjected to stretching and contracting exercises. Bhujaṅgāsana, Śalabhāsana and Dhanurāsana are fine stretching exercises for the front abdominal muscles, and serve as contracting exercises for the back muscles. Yoga- Mudrā, Paśchimatāna and Halāsana require vigorous contraction of the front abdominal muscles and put the back muscles on a very healthy stretch. What these six poses do for the front and back muscles of the abdomen, is done by Vakrāsana and Ardha-Matsyendrāsana for the side abdominal muscles. Śalabhāsana very vigorously exercises the diaphragm. Thus it will be clear that Āsana can give an efficient exercise to all abdominal muscles and enable them to carry out the automatic massage of the viscera very effectively.

However, when we take into consideration Uḍḍiyāna and Nauli, we see the real beauty of the Yogic exercises. Uḍḍiyāna gives a vertical massage to the abdominal organs. One can see with his own eyes the abdominal viscera slipping up and down behind the front abdominal muscles and thus getting themselves massaged vertically. Nauli gives a lateral massage to the abdominal organs. The two contracted recti roll from side to side across the whole expanse of the abdomen several times a minute, giving all the viscera lying behind them a massage the efficacy of which is simply surprising. No impartial student of the different systems of health culture can resist the conclusion that Uḍḍiyāna and Nauli have no parallel in any other system and that the Yogic seers have taken the best care of the abdominal muscles.

The strength of the abdominal muscles is useful not only in giving an automatic massage to the viscera, but it is also of a singular importance in keeping the abdominal organs in their proper places. These organs are either loosely hanging in the cavity of the abdomen or are feebly attached to its back wall. Thus they require a very strong support from the front. Otherwise they become displaced downwards and lead to various disorders, and to dyspepsia in particular. Now this front support is offered by the front abdominal muscles and its strength is proportionate to the strength of these muscles. By keeping the front abdominal muscles strong and elastic, Yogic poses not only give the automatic massage to the abdominal organs, but they hold all the abdominal viscera in their proper places and thus ensure proper digestion and absorption. When is done the part to be played by the digestive system in supplying the tissues all over the body with proteins, fats, salts and sugars is satisfactorily discharged.

The other system vitally connected with the supply of nourishment to the tissues is the circulatory system, because the work of carrying nutrition to the different tissues is done by the blood circulating through the human body. The circulatory system consists of the organs responsible for the circulation of the blood, namely, the heart, the arteries, the veins and the capillaries. Let us now examine the help Yogic poses render to this circulatory system.

The most important organ of blood circulation is the heart, because it is the contraction and relaxation of the heart that circulates the blood throughout the human body. The heart is made of the strangest muscular stuff, but it can always be made healthier by means of proper Yogic exercises. Uḍḍiyāna and Nauli raise[1] the diaphragm so high that they give a very good massage to the perpetually working heart from below. Again one of the ways of promoting the health of a muscle is to subject it to an alternate increase and decrease of pressure. The heart muscle is situated in the mediastinal cavity. Hence any increase or decrease of pressure in this cavity is shared by the heart. Now in Uḍḍiyāna and Nauli[2] the heart is alternately subjected to a decrease of pressure and thus gets an opportunity for building a healthier muscle. Again Bhujaṅgāsana, Śalabhāsana and Dhanurāsana alternately exert an increase pressure on the heart and the same thing is done by the first stages of Sarvāṅgāsana, Viparīta Karaṇī and Halāsana. This alternate increase and decrease of pressure brought about by the different Āsana promote the health of the heart and thus add to the efficiency of the circulatory system.

Out of all the organs of blood circulation the veins are the weakest, and yet they have to collect the blood from nearly the whole of the human body and raise it to the heart against the force of gravity. It is this uphill task that puts a very heavy strain on the weak structure of the veins and is responsible for such troubles as varicose veins. It is, therefore, the veins that stand in greater need of external help for preserving their health than any other part of the circulatory system. Yogic seers have found out a very easy way of helping these veins. They have invented Śīrṣāsana, Sarvāṅgāsana, Viparīta Karaṇī in which because of the upside-down position of the human body, the veins are enable to drain themselves into the heart without the least exertion on their part. The veins are very substantially relieved from the pressure of the blood flowing through them. The result is wonderful.

---

1. For studying the position of the diaphragm in Uḍḍiyāna and Nauli, vide Yoga Mīmāṁsā, Vol. III.
2. For pressure changes in the thorax during different Yogic exercises, vide Yoga Mīmāṁsā, Vol. IV.

The short relief that the veins get because of these Āsanas is so effective in preserving and even recovering the health of the veins, that patients suffering from varicose veins can get over their trouble by practicing these Āsanas for a few minutes every day. In this way, the veins being helped to better health and the heart being rendered healthier for the massage, the whole circulatory system satisfactorily performs its function of carrying proteins, fats, sugars and salts to all the tissues constituting the different parts of the human body.

The fifth element of nourishment is oxygen. Like the other four elements of nourishment this element is also carried to the tissues by the circulatory system. And as we have seen that the practice of Āsanas keeps the circulatory system healthy, we feel convinced that there would be no difficulty in feeding the tissues with oxygen, once it is taken up by the blood in the necessary quantity. Proteins, fats, sugars and salts are taken by the blood current from the digestive system. Oxygen is, however, taken from the respiratory system. We have, therefore, to see whether Āsanas can keep even the respiratory system in an efficient condition.

As must have been seen from the first chapter, the principal organ of respiration are the lungs. Satisfactory breathing activity does not, however, depend only upon the health of the lungs. Respiratory muscles play a very important part in this activity. They must be strong and healthy. Again the passage through which the lungs draw fresh air from the atmosphere, must be clear, so that the full breathing capacity of the lungs may be utilized in providing the system with oxygen. Thus we see that three conditions should be satisfied before the circulatory system gets the required amount of oxygen: (i) The lungs must be healthy. (ii) The respiratory muscles must be strong. (iii) The respiratory passage must be clear. Let us see whether the practice of Āsana can satisfy all these conditions in the case of a student of Yoga.

Broadly speaking, the health of the lungs depends upon the degree of their elasticity and upon the activity of the air-cells that go to compose them. If the lungs remain fully elastic and no air-cell in them remain idle, the health of the lungs can be taken to be ensured. Do the Āsanas render the lung tissue elastic and get every air-cell to take an active part in breathing? Yes, they do. The two Āsanas Śalabha and Mayūra have very great efficacy in this direction. Śalabhāsana requires deep inhalation and retention of breath for a few seconds at least under a high pulmonic pressure. This high pressure forces air into every cell of the lungs and opens it out for active work. A few turns in Śalabhāsana taken every day would allow no air-cell remain idle even in ordinary respiration, because once an air-cell is made habitual to take part in respiration, it does not easily lapse in to inactivity whether the pressure is low or high. What is true of Śalabhāsana, is also true of Mayūrāsana, as will be clear from the technique of the two poses give in the chapter on the cultural poses. The difference between Śalabhāsana and Mayūrāsana in this regard is as follows. In the former Kumbhaka is absolutely necessary whereas in the latter it is optional. The option of Kumbhaka in the practice of Mayūrāsana is due to the fact that a trained student of Yoga can balance himself in Mayūrāsana even without retaining his breath. Thus we see that Śalabhāsana and Mayūrāsana are quite capable of bringing every air-cell into its normal activity. Again Śalabhāsana is equally useful in keeping the lungs tissue fully elastic. As every medical man knows that an elastic tissue retains its complete elasticity if it is fully stretched at least a few times every day. As Śalabhāsana requires deep inspiration and retention of breath, during the practice of this Āsana, lungs are stretched out to their fullest extent. If Śalabhāsana is repeated three to seven times daily, the exercise will be quite sufficient for keeping the lungs fully elastic. Thus it is evident that complete elasticity of the lung tissues and fully activity of their air-cells, can be satisfactorily maintained by a student of Yogic poses.

Regarding the second condition - the strength of the respiratory muscles - deep inspiration required in Śalabhāsana and the deep expiration necessary in Uḍḍiyāna and Nauli, build powerful respiratory muscles, thus satisfactorily fulfilling the second condition upon which adequate supply of oxygen to the circulatory system depends.

Next we turn to the third condition - clearness of the respiratory passage. This passage at times becomes obstructed because of inflamed tonsils, adenoids, polypus, chronic nasal catarrh and deviated septum. Can the practice of Āsanas keep these obstructions away? Āsanas can surely deal with tonsils and in many cases even with chronic nasal catarrh. But against the other forms of obstructions Āsanas are powerless. Sarvāṅgāsana, Viparīta Karaṇī, Matsyāsana, Jihvā-Bandha and Siṃha-Mudrā[1] have been found very useful in treating cases of tonsillitis. Chronic nasal catarrh also very often[2] yields to these exercises. So if we exclude the few cases of adenoids, polypus and serious deviation of the septum, we find Āsanas are quite capable of keeping the respiratory passage clear.

1. For Siṃha-Mudrā of the Symbol of Lion, vide foot note 1, on p.100.

2. Nasal catarrh can be successfully treated by means of the different types of Neti and breathing exercises taught in Yoga.

Summing up our discussion about the three conditions upon the fulfilment of which depends the adequate supply of oxygen through the respiratory system, we see that Yogic poses do satisfy these conditions. Again, as has already been proved, these poses ensure the health of the circulatory system which carries this oxygen to the tissues. That means everything necessary for an adequate supply of proteins, fats, salts, sugars and oxygen to the tissues is done by the Āsanas for a student of Yoga.

As stated in the beginning of the chapter, the health of the tissues depends upon the adequate supply not only of these five elements of nourishment but also of the internal secretions of the endocrine glands. We have, therefore, to examine the efficacy of Āsanas in preserving the health of these endocrine structures. The thyroid, the pituitary, the pineal, the adrenals, the testes in the case of males and the ovaries in the case of females, may be looked upon as the most important of the various endocrine glands in the human body. Deficiency of secretion of any of these glands in the human body has been found to lead to serious consequences. Can Āsanas keep these endocrine glands healthy? The answer is surely in the affirmative. Sarvāṅgāsana, Viparīta Karaṇī, Matsyāsana, Jihva-Bandha and Siṃha-Mudrā have been found to be excellent exercise for the thyroid. The pituitary and the pineal glands are best taken care of by Śīrṣāsana. So far as the adrenals are concerned, Bhujaṅgāsana, Dhanurāsana, Uḍḍiyāna and Nauli are capable of preserving their health. For making the testes and the ovaries healthy Sarvāṅgāsana, Uḍḍiyāna and Nauli have been observed to have great efficacy. Thus it will be see that the practice of Āsanas can ensure the health of the most important endocrine glands and they can be made to supply the necessary secretions to the tissues.

This rapid survey of the physiological effects of Āsanas proves beyond all doubt that they amply satisfy the first condition upon which the health of the tissues depends, namely, a constant supply of proper nutrition and the internal secretions of the endocrine glands.

The second condition, which needs to be satisfied for maintaining the health of the tissues, is the effective removal of the waste products. Let us now study what these waste products are and whether Āsanas help the human body in effectively throwing them out.

The following may be stated to be the waste products. Carbon dioxide, uric acid, urea, bile, urine containing uric acid and urea, and the faecal matter containing bile along with undigested and indigestible matter from the food-stuffs. Most of these waste products are poisonous and if allowed to linger in the body unnecessarily, lead to serious disorders. It is, therefore, of utmost importance for the health of the tissues that they are properly excreted from the human body. Out of the different waste products, carbon dioxide is eliminated by the respiratory system, the urine containing uric acid and urea is discharged by the urinary system and the faecal matter containing bile along with the refuse of the foodstuff, is excreted by the digestive system. It is, therefore, evident that the waste products can be effectively removed from the body if only the three systems, namely, the respiratory, the urinary and the digestive, are able to function quite satisfactorily. While studying the question of nutrition, we have seen that the Yogic poses coupled with Uḍḍiyāna and Nauli, can keep the respiratory and the digestive system in an efficient condition. We find that Āsanas can take equal care of the urinary system. As stated in the first chapter, this system consists of the kidneys, the ureters, the bladder, and the urethra. Out of these the organ which really excretes urine is the kidneys, while others merely afford a sort of passage for the urine to leave the body. Now these kidneys are situated in the abdomen, and we have seen that some of the Āsanas are very fine abdominal exercises. When these Āsanas are supplemented by Ext remarkably high, and they are found to be quite competent to preserve the health of the kidneys. This being done the body is enabled satisfactorily to get rid of urine along with uric acid and urea which two substances the urine holds in solution.

In this way Āsanas have been found to satisfy the second physiological condition upon which the health of the tissues depends, namely, the effective removal of waste products.

Now we come to the study of the third and the last condition. It requires healthy functioning of nerve-connections. Let us first understand what is meant by the expression "healthy functioning of nerve connections", and then we shall try to see whether Āsanas can bring it about.

The most important part of the nervous system is the brain. Next to it is the spinal cord, and the two cords of the sympathetic. From the brain and from the spinal cord different nerves start branching off several times, and spread themselves to all the parts of the human body. The network of nerves thus prepared is so complete that there is not a single tissue in the human body that has not got its own nerve-connection. It is mainly because of their nerve-connections that

that the tissues are able to perform their work. If these nerve-connections degenerate, the function of the tissues also degenerates and if nerve connections are completely destroyed, the tissues do not function at all. Thus if the nerve supplying the colon degenerates, the tissues of the colon will not work and constipation will be the result. If one of the facial nerves is cut off, or becomes paralyzed, the muscles of the cheek supplied by that nerve, will not contract, but will remain perpetually in a relaxed condition, thus allowing the muscles of the other cheek to pull the face towards themselves, giving it the typical appearance presently by the patients of facial paralysis. Thus we see that the tissues of the human body will remain healthy and active only if the nerves connected with them are in a healthy condition. Hence, the third condition required for the health of the tissues, is the satisfactory functioning of their nerve-connections.

Can Āsanas keep the nervous mechanism of the whole body in an efficient condition? Yes, they can, Śīrṣāsana and Viparīta Karaṇī by sending a richer blood supply to the brain, ensure its health and also the health of the cranial nerves supplying the different organs of senses. All the Yogic poses are excellent spinal exercises. By giving the spine forward and backward bends and also right and left twists, Āsanas ensure perfect elasticity for it and lead to the health of the spinal cord which is held within the spinal column and also to the health of the two cords of the sympathetic, which lie imbedded in the muscles round about the spine. Uḍḍiyāna and Nauli operating through the diaphragm are of special value in promoting the health of the spinal cord and also of the sympathetic cords. As for the nerves issuing from the brain and the spinal cord, they lie for the most part in the chest and the abdomen. As already noticed, Āsanas, along with Uḍḍiyāna and Nauli, provide excellent exercises for both these parts of the human trunk and thus promote the health of the nerves lying within them. Śalabhāsana, Ardha-Śalabhāsana and the first parts of Sarvāṅgāsana, and Viparīta Karaṇī take care of the nerves of the lower extremities, whereas the part played by the upper extremities, in the technique of Śalabhāsana, Mayūrāsana, Sarvāṅgāsana, Viparīta Karaṇī etc., preserve the health of the nerves supplying them. Thus Āsanas are found capable of preserving the health not only of the brain and the spinal and sympathetic cords, but also of all the cranial and spinal nerves spreading throughout the body.

In this way our readers must have seen that all the three physiological conditions necessary for the health of the tissues can be thoroughly satisfied by the practice of Āsanas. Constant supply of proper nutrition and the internal secretions can be made available to the tissues all over the human body, waste products of all sorts can be effectively thrown out of the system, and all nerve-connections can be kept healthily functioning. All these conditions being satisfactorily fulfilled every tissue in the body is rendered healthy, yielding the maximum vigour to the whole organism of which it is capable. As the different systems working in the human body are made up of these tissues, every system discharges its function quite efficiently, thus producing perfect physiological harmony which ensures health and which yields the highest organic vigour.

In the last but one paragraph we have seen how Āsanas are peculiarly capable of training the spinal cord and the brain. These are the most important parts of the nervous system, and the spiritual force of Kuṇḍalinī when awakened works through them. If the brain or the spinal cord are not in a healthy condition and do not possess the strength necessary for sustaining the action of Kuṇḍalinī, a student of Yoga very often has to pass through a variety of troubles. Hence the extreme desirability of educating the brain and the spinal cord in the case of people who want to develop themselves spiritually through Yogic practices. That is why the training given through the cultural poses both to the brain and the spinal cord, is of special value to a spiritual culturist. Even in the cases of individuals who look to Yoga only for their physical health, the training of the brain and the spinal cord has a special significance. As seen in the first chapter of this handbook, all the systems working in the human body are controlled by the nervous system. And as the brain and the spinal cord are the most important parts of the nervous system and as upon their health depends the health and satisfactory functioning of the other parts of that system, the education of the brain and the spinal cord is as much essential to a student of health culture as to a spiritual culturist.

We cannot close this survey of the cultural poses before saying a word about the skeletal muscles. Not only all the physical activities of an individual but also his very health depends upon these skeletal muscles. If the hands and legs have no muscles or have defective muscles, no physical work will become possible. Again if the muscles of the chest and the abdomen degenerate, man would become a prey of various ills. Weak abdominal and pelvic muscles in the females are often responsible for the alarmingly large maternal mortality and the surprisingly large number of miscarriages in India. This will clearly show the importance of the skeletal muscles. Do Āsanas educate these skeletal muscles? The answer is both in the affirmative and in the negative. So far as the thoracic and abdominal muscles are concerned, Yogic poses do train them quite satisfactorily.

Hence a habitual student of Yogic poses will have no difficulty either in respiration or in digestion; and if the student is a female, she can be sure of healthy pregnancy and safe delivery. But the Yogic poses are not calculated to develop strong muscles for the arms or the legs. In the Yogic poses, there is ample provision of exercises that would preserve and promote the health of the muscles of the upper and lower extremities, but so far as strength is concerned, there is no special provision for it in Yogic Physical Culture. People whose profession requires muscular arms and legs must look to some other[1] system for training the muscles of these parts. It must, however, be borne in mind that the ordinary muscular needs of a civil life are entirely satisfied by the Yogic poses, whatever part of the human body the muscles may belong to.

Thus far we have surveyed somewhat rapidly the scientific features of the cultural poses. Now we wish to do the same thing regarding the meditative poses.

As pointed out in the beginning of this chapter, the object of the meditative poses is to offer a comfortable posture to the student of Yoga for Prāṇāyāma, Dhāraṇā and Samādhi; and in co-ordination with other Yogic exercises to help him in the awakening of Kuṇḍalinī. Let us now examine the physiology of these meditative poses and see whether that physiology can bring about this object.

If we study the meditative poses, we are at once struck by three physiological features which are so characteristic of them. These features may be stated as under.

(i) Erect position of the spine with a view to eliminate the possibility of the compression of the abdominal viscera and also to free the mind from the burden of the body.

(ii) A richer blood supply for the pelvic region toning up the coccygeal and sacral nerves and helping the awakening of Kuṇḍalinī in co-ordination with other Yogic practices.

(iii) Minimum production of carbon dioxide in the body, resulting in slowing the activity of the lungs and the heart, and excluding the body consciousness from the concentrating mind.

---

1. The dynamic form which we have given to the Yogic exercises and which has now been introduced by the U. P. Government in their educational institutions, is free from the shortcoming that is pointed out in these lines. Hence people who are keen on having muscular arms and legs, should take to this dynamic form of Yogic exercises. A text book of these exercises had already been published in Hindi and can be had from the Yoga Mimamsā Office.

Let us now examine these features in some details.

Every meditative pose requires the spine to be kept erect. We have, however, seen in the first chapter that naturally the spinal column is not quite straight, but has two convenient bends in its length. So when we talk of keeping the spine erect, we only mean that no new curves are to be introduced in the spinal column. This straight spine is secured by holding the trunk and the head perpendicular to the ground. The physiological advantage of keeping the spine erect, is very often pointed out to be that it keeps the spinal cord erect and thus keeps it in its proper place and allow it to function properly. This sort of argument does not appeal to us for the following reasons. First of all the spinal cord will not be quite straight, but will maintain its natural curve which it has to experience owing to the curved shape of the vertebral column in which it is held. Again the anatomical provisions for the protection of the spinal cord, are so thorough that there is no possibility of any interference with its functional activity, on account of any curves that the spinal column may be made to experience. Without entering into details we might note here that the spinal cord is invested by three membranes, and is surrounded by an amount of fluid, and also a considerable amount of fatty tissue that serves as a packing material. Thus the cord is supported in the canal by its membranes; and by means of them and of the fluid and packing of fatty tissue, it is protected from shocks and jars. When the vertebral column undergoes curves and twists, of course within particular limits, it is this protective arrangement inside the canal that keeps the cord safe and sound. So there is no chance of any interference with the functional activity of the spinal cord, even if the spine is not kept erect. Thus we see that the physiological advantage alleged to accrue from the maintenance of an erect spine, is more or less imaginary, and we have to seek the advantage elsewhere.

We are inclined to think that Yogic texts insist upon an erect posture in meditation, in order to avoid the compression of the abdominal viscera and the consequent train of diseases due to their congestion. In one of the foregoing paragraph we have seen how weak abdominal muscles lead to constipation. Now the relaxed posture which must result from the forward bend of the spine, if it is maintained for hours every day, as it would be maintained by a serious student of meditation, renders the abdominal muscles weak by being kept in a relaxed condition habitually. This along with the compression of the abdominal organs due to the stooping posture, leads to constipation, which in its turn gives rise to a number of ailments of a more or less dangerous character. All these troubles can be avoided if a man maintains an erect posture. And as this erect posture is secured by keeping the spine straight, Yogic texts require an erect vertebral column as a part of technique of the meditative poses.

There is another reason also why during meditation the spine is required to be held erect. During the period of meditation, the mind must be entirely relieved of the burden of the body. That means that the body must be given a posture which would be at once easy, comfortable and balanced. Now all these advantages are secured in the meditative poses because of the erect spine, the broad triangular base prepared by the folded legs and the hands that rest either on the knees or on the heels arranged in front of the pelvis. If we exclude the horizontal position assumed by the spine when we lie down, erect position is the most comfortable that the spinal column can maintain. The horizontal position is not available for Yogic meditation, because in that position the student stands the danger of falling asleep. So erect position is the only position available for meditation. Students who practice meditation find the meditative poses extremely comfortable, leaving the mind free to follow its own activities, without being disturbed by the body.

The second physiological feature of the meditative poses is their capacity to keep a richer blood supply playing about the pelvic region and thus to tone up the coccygeal and sacral nerves. In all these poses flexors of the lower extremities are greatly contracted and pressed. The remaining muscles lie inactive across a considerable length of time. Owing of these reasons the free current of blood circulation is interfered with. This provides the pelvic region with a larger blood supply from the bifurcation of the abdominal aorta. Consequently, the nerves that issue from this part of the vertebral column, namely, the coccygeal and sacral nerves, get the advantage of this richer blood supply and are toned up.

This increased blood supply and the consequent toning up of the nerves, is to some extent responsible for the awakening of Kuṇḍalinī, of course when other Yogic exercises for rousing Kuṇḍalinī are coordinated with these meditative poses. This conclusion is based upon the view expressed in some traditions that a continued practice of the meditative poses is in itself sufficient to awaken Kuṇḍalinī.

Tho third and the last physiological feature that we have to consider is the minimum production of carbon dioxide. This minimum production of carbon dioxide is due to the fact that these poses involve a very small amount of muscular activity. Although the muscular energy required for maintaining the meditative poses, is not so small as that spent in lying down or in sleeping, yet it can be safely maintained that out of all the poses assumed in sitting or standing, the meditative poses entail the least expenditure of muscle energy. Owing to this circumstance the production of carbon dioxide during the maintenance of the meditative poses, is also reduced to the minimum.

Now it is an acknowledged physiological fact that the activity of the lungs is proportionate to the production of carbon dioxide in the body. If large quantities of carbon dioxide are manufactured in the body, the activity of the lungs is largely increased, as when athletes are engaged in running, wrestling, rowing, etc. On the contrary the movements of the lungs become very slow, if carbon dioxide is produced on a small scale in the body, as is done when persons are lying down or sleeping. Again the action of the heart keeps pace with the action of the lungs. When the action of the lungs is exaggerated, cardiac activity also slows down. According to these physiological facts, when the production of carbon dioxide is minimized during the meditative poses, both the lungs and the heart have a tendency to slow down their speed. When these meditative poses are maintained across a considerable length of time, say even for half an hour at a stretch, breathing becomes so shallow and the heart beats become so controlled, that all the activities of the student appear to have come to a standstill. Under these circumstances breathing becomes exclusively abdominal; and it is only the slightly backward and forward movements of the abdominal muscles that reveal the working of the lungs to a careful observer. Such being the case the mind of the Yogic student ceases almost entirely to be disturbed by physical movements, voluntary and involuntary; and he finds himself free first to direct his mind inward to fathom its own mysteries, then to isolate himself even from his mental equipment and stand face to face with Reality, into which he merges at last and with which he becomes ultimately identified.

This short, scientific survey of Yogic poses drives us irresistibly to the conclusion that the advantages claimed for Āsanas are fully justified, and that no man wishing to develop his body, mind and soul by taking to the practice of only one system of exercises, can afford to overlook Āsanas.

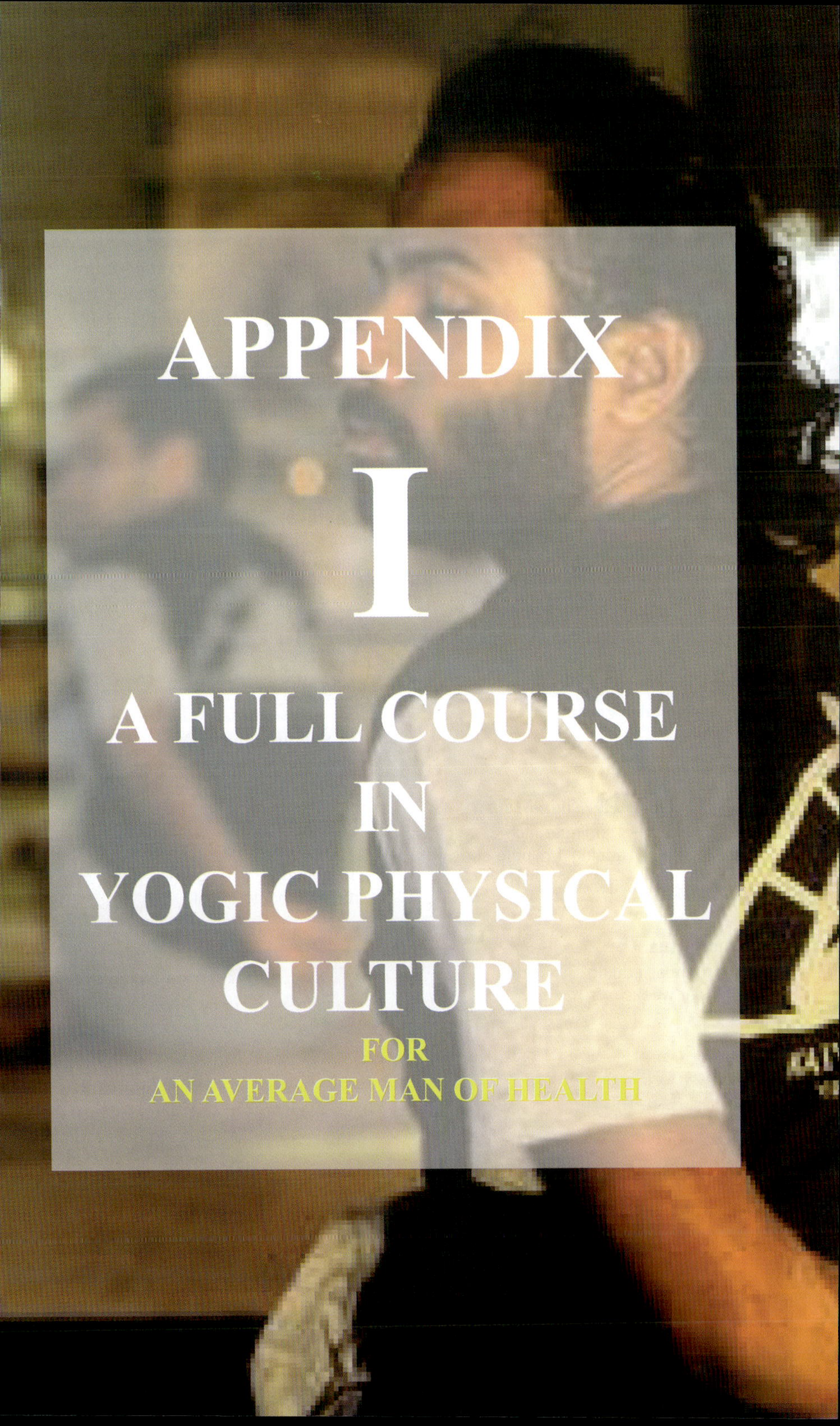

APPENDIX I

A FULL COURSE IN YOGIC PHYSICAL CULTURE

FOR AN AVERAGE MAN OF HEALTH

Start Here >

1 Śīrṣāsana
15 seconds to 12 minutes, adding 30 seconds per week.

2 Sarvāṅgāsana
30 seconds to 6 minutes, adding 1 minute per week.

3 Matsyāsana
15 seconds to 3 minutes, adding 15 seconds per week.

4 Halāsana
1 minute to 4 minutes, for all stages together, adding 1 minute per week.

5 Bhujaṅgāsana
3 to 7 rounds of each, the pose being maintained.

6 Śalabhāsana
10 seconds, adding 1 round every fortnight.

7 Dhanurāsana
10 seconds, adding one round every fortnight.

8 Ardha-Matsyendrāsana
15 seconds to 1 minute, adding 15 seconds per week.

9 Paśchimatāna
15 seconds to 1 minute, adding 15 seconds per week.

10 Mayūrāsana
10 seconds to 2 minutes, adding 15 seconds per week.

11 Śavāsana
2 minutes to 10 minutes, adding 2 minutes per week.

12 Uḍḍiyāna
3 to 7 rounds, adding 1 round per week.

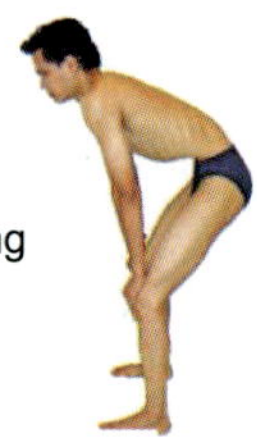

13 Yoga-Mudrā
1 minute to 3 minutes, adding 1 minute per week.

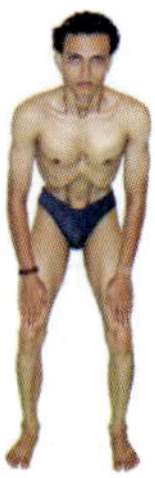

14 Nauli
3 to 7 rounds, adding 1 round per week.

15 Kapālabhāti
3 rounds of 11 to 121 expulsions each, adding 11 expulsions to each round every week

16 Ujjāyī
7 to 28 rounds, adding 3 rounds every week.

17 Bhastrikā
3 rounds of 11 to 121 expulsions each, adding 11 expulsions to each round every week. Every round to be followed by a suitable Kuṁbhaka.

A FEW HINTS REGARDING THE FULL COURSE

LIMITATIONS

- Students to Yogic Physical Culture will do well to remember the limitations that have been indicated from time to time in Yoga Mīmāṁsā for each exercise; and which have been summarized here in the following section.

- People suffering from running ears, weak eye capillaries and weak heart should avoid the practice of Śīrṣāsana. This, Viparīta Karaṇī and Sarvāṅgāsana, may be very cautiously practiced by those that are troubled by chronic nasal catarrh. Bhujaṅgāsana, Śalabhāsana and Dhanurāsana are to be avoided by persons with considerable tenderness in the abdominal viscera, especially when the spleen is excessively enlarged. Constipated people will be well advised not to practice Yoga-Mudrā and Paśchimatāna on a large measure. Generally speaking weakness in the heart should exclude the exercises of Uḍḍiyāna, Nauli, Bhastrikā and Kapālabhāti. Weakness in the lungs also indicates the exclusion of Kapālabhāti as well as Bhastrikā and Ujjāyī Kumbhakas, although the Recaka and Pūraka of Ujjāyī are available even to people with weak lungs. Persons recording blood pressure above 150 and below 100 mm. Hg. habitually, should exclude the Yogic exercises altogether, provided they are going to undertake these exercises on their own responsibility.

N. B. - Any one suffering from considerable weakness in any part of the body will do well to consult an expert for giving him the necessary exercises.

MEASURE

- The course is perfectly general. The proportion of time shown against each exercise is also general and has no reference to individual cases.

- Students may stop short with only half the maximum time put down for each exercise, provided that they observe the relative proportion among the different practices.

- In Section 6 another alternative is shown.

- The maximum to be reached in the different exercises in the FULL COURSE, may also be as follows:

Śīrṣāsana	6 minutes
Sarvāṅgāsana	3 minutes
Matsyāsana	1 minute
Halāsana	2 minutes
Bhujaṅgāsana	3 minutes
Śalabhāsana	3 minutes
Dhanurāsana	3 minutes
Ardha-Matsyendrāsana	1 minute
Paśchimatāna	1 minute
Mayūrāsana	1 minute
Uḍḍiyāna	2 minutes
Yoga-Mudrā	1 minute
Nauli	3 minutes
Kapālabhāti or Bhastrikā	8 minutes
Ujjāyī	7 minutes

- People who want to reduce their time of exercise to the lowest possible minimum, should take up the SHORT COURSE.

CAUTION

- Under no circumstances should the exercises lead to languor. The student should come out of his practices fully refreshed, a sort of quiet settling over his nerves.

- The whole course need not be gone through at a stretch. It may be profitably punctuated with convenient periods of rest.

- Even then care should be taken to see that the total amount of energy expended does not strain the system.

- Be with caution bold is our repeated advised to the student of Yogic Physical Culture.

- If there is a considerable break in the practice of these exercises, whenever the exercises are to be started again, they should start on a humbler scale, although the full measure may be reached somewhat rapidly.

- After severe illness the Yogic exercises should be undertaken only when the patient recovers sufficient energy for their practice. It would always be desirable, by way of a cautious measure, to prefix to the practice of these exercises, a moderately long walk everyday for a week or so.

- Yogic exercises should never commence for an hour and a half after even a moderate quantity of solid food or a good quantity of liquid food. Half a cup of liquid food would allow the exercises to be started in half an hour. At least four hours and a half must elapse between a heavy meal and the Yogic exercises. In short, Yogic exercises should always begin with a light stomach.

- There is no harm if food is taken in a moderate quantity in something like half an hour after the Yogic exercises.

PLACE

- Any well ventilated place may be used for Yogic exercises. The only care to be taken is not to allow the body to be exposed to a strong draught.

SEAT

- For a spiritual culturist the traditional arrangement of seating is excellent. A carpet of Kuśa grass[1], with a well-tanned deer-hide spread on it, the hide in its turn being covered with a daily washed piece of thick khaddar, makes a very comfortable seat. A physical culturist may use a carpet large enough to accommodate the length and breadth of the individual practicing Yogic exercises. From the hygienic point of view it is desirable that this carpet also is covered with a daily washed piece of khaddar.

TIME AND SEQUENCE

- Uḍḍiyāna, Nauli, Kapālabhāti or Bhastrikā and Ujjāyī should be practiced in the morning, in the sequence in which they have been taken up here.

---

1. In the absence of a Kuśa grass carpet, any other grass carpet will do. Those that may have a conscientious objection to the use of a hide should make use of a thick, woolen cloth folded over several times.

- Uḍḍiyāna and Nauli may be practiced by the constipated people even before they get the call of nature.

- Taking a few ounces, say ten to twenty, of tepid water, with a little rock salt added to it (1 grain per ounce), may be taken before practicing Nauli. This will induce a rapid bowel movement.

- Kapālabhāti or Bhastrikā and Ujjāyī should follow not only evacuation, but, as far as possible, a full bath. They are best practiced in Padmāsana or Siddhāsana although for Kapālabhāti and Bhastrikā, Padmāsana is preferable.

- Āsanas are better gone through in the evening, because muscles are more elastic then than in the morning.

- Yoga-Mudrā so also Ujjāyī and Kapālabhāti or Bhastrikā may be practiced also in the evening.

- Yoga-Mudrā should be taken up with Āsanas and be practiced before Śavāsana.

- Whether in the morning or in the evening, the Yogic exercises should be practiced in the following order. First take Āsanas with Yoga - Mudrā, then the Bandha and the Kriyas, and lastly the Prāṇāyāmas. Kapālabhāti should be considered as a part of Prāṇāyāma.

- In practicing Āsanas students will do well to preserve the sequence of the various poses that has been followed in enlisting them here. In getting oneself trained, however, one need not follow this order he likes, the easiest being taken up first and the more difficult being taken up later on.

- The omission of a particular practice does not disqualify a student to go through the remaining part of the scheme with advantage.

COMBINATION WITH OTHER EXERCISES

- There is no harm in undergoing the Yogic exercises and strenuous muscular exercises side by side.

- But the two should never be practiced immediately before one another.

At least a period of twenty minutes should be allowed to go by.

- Those that want to finish their exercises with a balance introduced into their system, should take the Yogic exercises last. But those that want to have a spirit of exhilaration at the end, should finish with the muscular exercises.

- Walk when taken as an exercise must be brisk, and for considerations of sequence should be treated as a muscular exercise. A stroll stands on a different level, and may precede or follow the Yogic practices.

YOGIC EXERCISES AND BATH

- A whole bath should precede the Yogic exercises. Because the same promotes blood circulation uniformly throughout the body, and the diversion of a richer blood current to a particular part by means of a Yogic exercise becomes easier.

- But a local bath intended for a particular part of the body for promoting blood circulation therein, should neither precede nor follow the general Yogic exercises may be combined with the advice of an expert.

FOOD, DRINK, SMOKE, ETC.

- Every man should try to find which food suits him the best, irrespective of the dictates of his palate.

- Even people who maintain more than average health, should restrict themselves to such varieties of food as they find agreeable. Every meal should be of moderate quantity which must be well masticated, so that it may become freely mixed with the salive and its digestion may become easier.

- People with weak digestion should take to low protein diet. They should satisfy themselves with two meals per day and preferably even with one, the place of the other meal being taken by light refreshment.

- Those who suffer from dyspepsia and constipation or have some uric acid trouble, will do well to eliminate all sorts of pulse. They should also avoid potatoes, brinjals and onions.

- Water taken half an hour after the meal suits almost every constitution. Those that have their digestive capacity unimpaired may take water along with their food.

- All alcoholic drinks are to be cautiously avoided. Stimulants such as tea and coffee are never to be taken in excess and may preferably be eliminated altogether. For a man who cares for his health, there cannot be a more luxurious drink than plain water.

- Heavy smoking of whatever sort invariably shatters the nerves, if carried on across many years. Weak nerves, persistent cough, sore throat, etc., always harass smoker; and may often beset the path even of a light smoker.

- All unnatural and illegitimate sexual acts are sinful. Excess committed even in natural and legitimate sexual acts do not stand upon a different footing.

- No sexual intercourse is healthy unless it is undertaken as a matter of absolute physiological necessity.

EXERCISES FOR FEMALES

- The FULL COURSE is available to females as well as to males.

- In the case of females it is desirable to suspend all the Yogic exercises during the monthly illness and pregnancy.

EXERCISES FOR BOYS AND GIRLS

- Boys and girls will do well, first to start with the SHORT COURSE in every case and to take up the FULL COURSE later on.

- Boys and girls under 12 would be well advised to restrict themselves to Bhujaṅgāsana, Ardha-Śalabhāsana, Dhanurāsana, Paśchimatāna, Halāsana and Yoga Mudrā only. After the age of 12 the remaining exercises of the FULL COURSE may be taken up.

N.B. This FULL COURSE and the hints given thereon are intended for an average man of health. People falling below the average may try the SHORT COURSE, or better seek expert advice, for being prescribed suitable exercises.

APPENDIX II

A SHORT COURSE IN YOGIC PHYSICAL CULTURE

Start Here >

1 Bhujaṅgāsana

3 to 7 turns each; the pose being maintained for 2 to 5 seconds, one turn being added to each, every fortnight.

2 Ardha-Śalabhāsana

3 to 7 turns each; the pose being maintained for 2 to 5 seconds, one turn being added to each, every fortnight.

3 Dhanurāsana

3 to 7 turns each; the pose being maintained for 2 to 5 seconds, one turn being added to each, every fortnight.

4 Halāsana

First only Ardha-Halāsana to be tried for two seconds in each of its stages. Then the full pose may be taken through its four different stages, each stage being maintained for 2 seconds only. 3 to 5 turns, adding one turn every fortnight.

5 Paśchimatāna

To be maintained for 5 seconds. 3 to 7 turns, adding one turn every fortnight.

6 Ardha-Matsyendrāsana

To be maintained for 5 seconds. 3 to 5 turns, adding one turn every fortnight.

7 Yoga-Mudrā

To be maintained for 10 seconds. 3 to 5 turns, adding one turn per week.

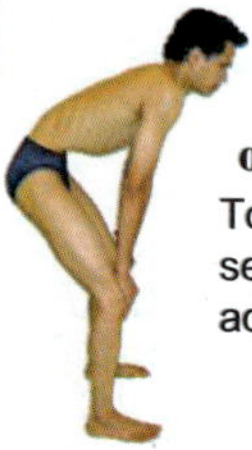

or Uḍḍiyāna

To be maintained for 10 seconds. 3 to 5 turns, adding one turn per week.

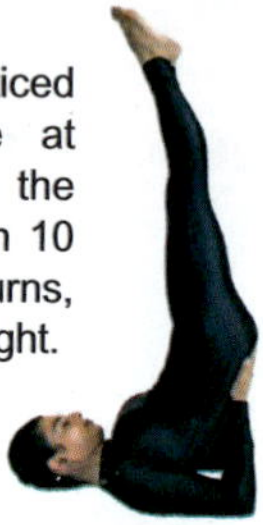

8 Viparīta Karaṇī

First Ardha to be practiced with 2 seconds pause at every stage. After-wards the full pose to be taken with 10 seconds pause. 2 to 5 turns, adding one turn very fortnight.

9 Ujjāyī

7 to 21 rounds, adding 3 rounds per week.

APPENDIX II

A FEW HINTS REGARDING THE SHORT COURSE

- The SHORT COURSE is framed for those people who cannot, for want of time, strength or wish, follow the FULL COURSE.

- All the hints given to Yogic Physical Culturists concerning the FULL COURSE should be applicable to this SHORT COURSE as well as to the EASY COURSE that follows.

- Exercises tabulated in the SHORT COURSE may be started at the age of 9. Ujjāyī and Uḍḍiyāna should nor be begun, however, before 12 or even 13.

- The SHORT COURSE is available to females as well as to males.

- Those that can tolerate Yogic exercises in the morning, may if they so choose, undergo the SHORT COURSE both morning and evening. Others should practice Ujjāyī and Uḍḍiyāna in the morning and the rest of the exercises in the evening. Ujjāyī is to be practiced in the evening scale.

- This SHORT COURSE may be made shorter not by omitting any of the practices tabled here, but by undergoing all the exercises on a smaller scale.

- Although the practice of the SHORT COURSE or of the EASY COURSE tabulated hereafter is comparatively innocent, people suffering from any serious disorder should not undertake exercises on their own responsibility.

- The EASY COURSE that follows is intended for those who are much run down in health and are suffering from general debility, but have no other specific complaint.

APPENDIX III

AN EASY COURSE IN YOGIC PHYSICAL CULTURE

Start Here >

1 Ujjāyī
7 to 14 rounds, adding 2 rounds per week.

2 Bhujaṅgāsana
2 to 5 turns each; the pose to be maintained for 2 to 5 seconds, one turn being added to each, every fortnight.

3 Ardha-Śalabhāsana
2 to 5 turns each; the pose to be maintained for 2 to 5 seconds, one turn being added to each, every fortnight.

4 Ardha-Halāsana
Begin with one leg only. To be practiced with both the legs after a fortnight. Rest for 2 seconds at angles of 15°, 30°, 60° and 90°; 3 to 6 turns, adding one turn every fortnight.

5 Vakrāsana
To be maintained for 5 seconds on each side. 3 to 6 turns, adding one turn every fortnight.

6 Chakrāsana (Side bending)
To be maintained for 2 seconds on each side. 2 to 5 turns, adding one turn every fortnight.

7 Paśchimatāna
To be maintained for 5 seconds. 3 to 5 turns, adding one turn every fortnight.

8 Yoga-Mudrā or its variations
To be maintained for 5 seconds. 3 to 5 turns, adding one turn per week.

APPENDIX IV

THE RATIONALE OF YOGIC POSES

by

Swami Kuvalayananda

Yoga Mīmāṁsā (J.G. Gune)

July 1926, Second Impression,

Vol. II No.3

The Rationale of Yogic Poses

Up to now we have noticed in the pages of this magazine the most important of the Yogic poses. Though only two of them have been studied at some length, the technique of nearly every pose mentioned in this journal has been detailed. We now propose, in this article, to examine the general principles underlying this part of Yogic Physical Culture.

As our research work is yet restricted to physiology and as we have not yet started collecting any experimental evidence on the objective side to substantiate Yogic claims in the field of psycho-physiology, our studies in this article will necessarily be limited to the physical culture and therapeutical sides of Yoga. We can only assure our readers that some of the Āsanas at least are capable of directly helping to rouse the spiritual forces, whereas there is not a single pose noticed in this journal that is not capable of indirectly leading to spiritual progress.

At the very outset it is to be made clear that the poses by themselves do not constitute the entire system of Yogic Physical Culture. They form only a fraction is greatly important. In order, therefore, to understand the rationale of Yogic poses, it is necessary not only to study the general principles underlying the Yogic system of Physical Culture as a whole, but also to have a hurried survey of the entire field of Physical Culture, noting the most salient points of comparison and contrast between the Yogic and non Yogic systems.

A system of Physical Culture means a system of bodily exercises such as are denuded of all utilities or ulterior ends except those of physical development. The word *gymnastics* is very often used as an equivalent of the science of Physical Culture. To our mind Gymnastics is a wider term and includes exercises which may not belong to a *system* of Physical Culture. An example will make matters clear. If we take into consideration the exercises on the parallel bars, we find that they do belong to Gymnastics, but they do not belong to a system of Physical Culture. For, a system of Physical Culture requires the exercises to be so planned and organized as would develop the different parts of the body in their due proportion and as would also build every part of the human body. It is not sufficient for exercises to belong to a system of Physical Culture that they are capable of helping the growth of some parts of bodily frame.

Now if we take the parallel bars exercises, we find that they do help body building; but it is only the upper part of the somatic frame that is developed and not the body as a whole. Hence the parallel bars cannot for a system of Physical Culture, although they do fall under Gymnastics.[1]

The idea of the science of Physical Culture as it is described in the preceding paragraphs is essentially a modern idea in the West. In ancient Greece and Rome body-building was, indeed, given the highest attention. The Greeks are more known for their philosophy than for their gymnastics. And yet physical culture was a veritable passion with them. Plato, one of the greatest Greek philosophers, considered weakness to be perilously near to wickedness and ugliness to sin! But even the ancient Greeks, physical culture was never studied by itself. It was always developed as a preparation for either games and sports or for military training. The athlete had always his eyes directed to the Pan-hellenic and especially to the Olympic games or to the fields of battle where he would fight in honour of his motherland. The ancient Romans were emphatically a military race. Hence gymnastics formed only a humble part of the science of war. From this it will be clear that in ancient Europe physical culture began to be cultivated as an independent science, advocating systems of exercises that would constitute entire schemes of for body-building complete in themselves.

Things obtaining in ancient India were not much different than those prevailing in ancient Europe. Here too body-building does not look to be practiced for itself; but it generally prepared the gymnast either for games or for war. The very word Malla-Vidyā which is commonly used to denote gymnastic exercises, means the science of wrestling. To the best of our knowledge, in ancient Saṅskṛta literature, there is no mention of an independent science taking care of body-building as such.

---

1. It may be interesting here to note the controversy which raged in Germany over the parallel bars in the middle of the nineteenth century. From the Royal Central Institute established in Berlin under the joint control of the ministers of war and education, the bars, horizontal as well as parallel, were banished. This was due to the strictly scientific attitude towards physical culture on the part of the head of the Institute. As, however, the bars belonged to gymnastics as it was being developed in Germany, the patriotic feelings rose so high that a very long and bitter controversy ensued in which gymnasts, medical men and university professors took an active part. At last a commission of the most eminent medical men was appointed, and they declared that the bars exercises from the medical point of view should not be excluded. It is to be borne in mind, however, that the commissioners did not declare the bar exercises to form a system of physical culture.

We cannot, however, afford to pass over one circumstance which may go against what we have said in the last paragraph. In non-medical Saṅskṛta literature there are references to physical exercise undergone as a daily routine independent of wrestling or any other game. It is called Vyāyāma which literally means stretching. This fact creates a strong suspicion in favour of the ancient Indians, crediting them with having a system of Physical Culture in the modern sense of the word. The suspicion grows almost into conviction when we look to the medical texts referring to bodies built through Vyāyāma as being immune from diseases. These texts also speak of Vyāyāma independent of Malla-Vidyā. The traditions of all the gymnasiums in India also strengthen this conviction. A fairly large number of students in Indian gymnastics institutes goes there simply for body-building, and never undergoes any training in games or sports.

What we have said in the last two paragraphs pertains to non-Yogic physical culture. Although we could not say anything very definitely in this connection, we have precise information bearing on Yogic Physical Culture. But before we pass on to it, we have to make a brief reference to a type of exercise which is nowadays paid much attention to in Mahārāshṭra and which is claimed, by its advocates, to be an entire system of Physical Culture. We mean the Namaskāras or prostrations before the Sun-god. This system of exercise has been in vogue in Mahārāshṭra at least for a few centuries and is very much favoured by the upper class of the society. In the eighteenth century it was not unusual to find youths making as many as twelve hundred prostrations every morning. Among such youths were to be seen some of the Brāhmaṇa rules of the land. In athletic tournaments recently held in Nāsika, there were competitors for as many as two thousand prostrations. Now as these prostrations form a part of Sun-worship, they can never be looked upon as a system of Physical Culture in the modern sense of the word, for the moderners require such a system to have no other end except that of body-building.

Coming to Yogic exercises for physical development, we have at once to admit that they were never meant for body-building exclusively. They were always prescribed for so training the body as would easily lead to spiritual development and would sustain the working of the spiritual forces when roused. Physical culture was invariably with the Yogins a step to spiritual culture. Hence if any of the Indian systems of Physical Culture least approaches the modern idea of the science, it is the Yogic system.

Even in India – the home of Yoga -- supreme ignorance prevails, especially in the educated circles, about Yoga in general and Haṭha Yoga in particular. The latter is looked upon as merely physical, having no spiritual counterpart at all! Nay, some of the critics go so far as to assert that Haṭha Yoga runs counter to spiritual life! This radically wrong concept of Haṭha Yoga is due to the want of direct knowledge either of the Yogic literature or of the Yogic tradition. No student of Yoga can take even his first lessons without undertaking to discipline his mind through Yamas and Niyamas. Even a Haṭha Yogin cares for his body simply because it is the only instrument through which he can reach his spiritual goal. We have to request our readers, with all the earnestness we can command, not to build their theories on the imperfect or misleading evidence obtained from mock Yogin who, like depraved tumblers, eke out a living by prostituting some of the physical exercises in Yoga.

So the fact is that the body-building exercises of Yoga never formed a system of Physical Culture in the modern sense of the word, as they were always designed for spiritual rather than for bodily development!

Here naturally the question arises as to why, in spite of the fact stated above, the Kaivalyadhama is trying to evolve a Yogic system of Physical Culture. We are going to take up this very question. But before we do so, we have to say a few words by way of further introduction.

Though the idea of physical culture as stated above is of modern growth, it does not mean that the physical culturists of today have created something altogether independent of the body-building exercises of the ancient people. The European and America systems of Physical Culture are a steady evolution of the Greek and Roman exercises. True, many features of the modern systems were totally absent from those of the olden days. True also, the striking advance made by anatomy and physiology during the last century has given physical culture a scientific air and completeness such as were never enjoyed by it before. But this does not disprove the fact that the modern systems of Physical Culture are a slow and systematic growth of the ancient bodily exercises obtaining in Greece and Rome.

What applies to Europe and America also holds good in the case of India. Here too physical culturists are busy developing different systems of body-building. In the absence of wild advertisement of the Western type, these systems have not yet attracted much attention of the Indian nation as a whole, and are naturally little known to people outside India. No serious attempt has yet been made to expound these systems by their founders. Some stray articles do appear here and there in the vernacular; but an orderly exposition is still to be undertaken for teaching these different systems of Indian Physical Culture. It is to be noted, however, that every one of these has its sphere of influence which in some cases is markedly extensive.

These Indian physical culturists also are freely using the material handed down by ancient tradition, for building up their respective systems. Knowledge of anatomy and physiology is largely utilized and the Western advance of physical culture is also taken into account. Already the traditional exercises for bodily development were scientifically sounds – much more sound than the modern scientific mind would ever suspect. Hence the edifice erected on this foundation is also likely to be sound. Among the non-yogic systems of Physical Culture the one that makes the nearest approach to a scientifically sound method, is the system founded by Prof. Manikrao of Baroda, at whose feet we had the proud privilege of sitting for our lessons in non-yogic physical culture, and to whose parental care we owe much that has made us what we are now.

Just like the Western physical culturists, the Indian founders of the different systems of Physical Culture, have freed the science from all ulterior ends and have placed it on an independent footing. The advocates of Namaskāras have, indeed, imported much from outside into their system; but as they have tried to accomplish everything within the narrow compass of one exercise and as they want to ever tack that exercise on to Sun-worship, there is little chance of their system ever being accepted as a system of Physical Culture in the modern sense of the word.[1]

This brief statement of the position of physical culture in olden and modern times, clearly shows that the science is being reconstructed in India as in the West. Attempts are being made to place it on an independent footing and to make it as complete as possible.

---

1. This statement has been made from a particular point of view and as such should not lead to misunderstanding. The exercise to Namaskāra, as it is being developed by its advocates, has a definite purpose to serve and has certainly a large scope in India. We wish them success from the bottom of our heart.

Even a cursory study of the modern progress of this science will bring into relief a few developments which cannot fail to attract the attention of the students of Yoga.

i) Every day the utility of breathing exercises is being realized to a greater and greater extent.
ii) Of all the systems working in the body the nervous system is recognized to be the most important.
iii) The spinal column is being assigned its legitimate place in the scheme of bodily exercises.
iv) A feeble but marked reaction has started against the disproportionate attention paid to muscle by physical culturists.
v) Exercises are being devised to preserve and promote the health of endocrine glands.

The Yogic tradition in India has very emphatically laid stress upon these very features of body-building for more than a score of centuries. True, the Yogins of old built their bodies simply to prepare themselves for spiritual life. But this does not deprive their exercises of the credit of being based on scientific principles the significance of which the modern physical culturist is but slowly realizing now. The western founders of the different systems of Physical Culture are, indeed, busily engaged in devising exercises for the spine, nerves and endocrine glands. But an impartial study of their attempts has convinced us that their exercises are, at best, a poor copy of the marvelous exercises of Yoga.[1]

By using the word copy, we never want to suggest that they are borrowing their exercises from Yoga. Almost all of them do not even mention the name of Yoga. And a few of them that mention it, give little credit to the Yogic system. We take all of them to be honest people acting up to their convictions. But when we go through the pages of their books and magazines, we come across exercises which are so strikingly similar to the Yogic exercises, that we cannot help noting the similarity and calling one the copy of the other. We may, however, put the matter in the form of another remark, the truth of which, we are sure, we will be able to prove up to the hilt. The Western physical culturists have invented exercises for the development of the spine, nerves

---

1. We are sincerely sorry for making this statement here. We are sorry not because the statement is hasty, nor yet because it is inaccurate; but simply because it has come too early so far as our publication of the evidence supporting it is concerned. We shall require years before we fully place before the public the evidence that we have collected even up to now. Every year our labours are largely adding to the original stock. We have to request our readers, therefore, not to take the statement on trust but to wait and scan our evidence as we produce it; and accept the truth of the statement only when they are convinced.)

and endocrine glands, which were anticipated, centuries before, by the Yogic seers, and which are far from reaching the efficacy of the Yogic exercises available for the same purpose.

The Indian physical culturists, including the advocates of Namaskāras, have tried their best to take advantage of their knowledge of Yoga. Every one of them is very particular in publicly declaring that his system has been based on Yogic exercises. Some of them even go to the length of warmly maintaining that their systems are composed purely of Yogic exercises. Of late, in Mahārāshṭra, there is not a single gymnastic institute worth the name, that does not undertake to teach Yogic Asanas. We are greatly pleased to see this attitude of the Indian physical culturists towards Yoga. But we are sorry to say that in most of the cases the fundamental principles underlying the Yogic system of Physical Culture are but imperfectly understood, and the combination of Yogic and non-Yogic exercises that these people are attempting, is something far from being scientifically satisfactory. As, however, the Indian physical culturists are maintaining a reverential attitude towards Yoga, there is every possibility of their one day fully and rightly utilizing the extremely valuable material available in Yogic culture.

Even at the risk of being a little irrelevant, we wish to say a few words to the physical culturists of India. Barring a few honorable exceptions, they are not as well equipped with the knowledge of modern sciences necessary for their work, as the Western people laboring in the same field are. The Western physical culturists are, day by day, bringing themselves into a closer touch with medical science, psychology, sociology, etc.; and the thoroughness with which they work, deserves our best congratulations. Their restless industry and untiring patience are virtues worth anybody's imitation. If all the physical culturists in India work with the patience, industry and thoroughness of their western brethren, Indian systems are sure to shine with greater glory, and come to occupy their legitimate positions among the systems of the world.

In the discussion preceding the last paragraph two points have been made out:

i) The science of physical culture in the modern sense of the word, is of recent growth in the West and most probably also in India. In making it independent and self-contained, it is being freed from its dependence upon games, military training, etc.

ii) In its reconstruction which is going on everywhere, it is tending to emphasize features which are characteristic of Yogic system of Physical Culture.

We are quite conscious that two questions must have been repeatedly troubling a skeptic reader of our journal and especially of this article. They are –

i) Whether the traditional Yoga-Vidyā had any system of Physical Culture according to the modern idea of the science?
ii) Whether evolving a Physical Culture system out of the traditional Yoga-Vidyā, is not prostituting the latter?

In one of the foregoing paragraphs we have very frankly admitted that the body-building exercises of Yoga never formed a system of Physical Culture in the modern sense of the word. This admission should not, however, be construed to mean that the Yogic exercises are not capable of being organized in such a way as would yield a self-contained and independent system of Physical Culture. After disposing off the second question raised above, we propose first to give a list of Yogic exercises that would go to form an entire system of Physical Culture, even in the modern sense of the word. We shall then notice some of the principles upon which an ideal system of Physical Culture should be based. And lastly we will examine the Yogic exercises, with a special reference to Asanas, and decide whether most of these principles underlie the Yogic exercises and whether these exercises have a claim to constitute a system of Physical Culture.

The second question we answer emphatically in the negative. To take advantage of a part of Yoga-Vidyā for a lower ideal is certainly not prostituting it. Picking up a few exercises and practicing them for physical culture exclusively would not bring into discredit the science of Yoga. On the contrary it should set a premium upon it. In our extensive therapeutic work in the field of Yoga, we have invariably seen that the patient's faith in Yoga as a system of spiritual culture is greatly strengthened by the bodily advantages he derives. We would be doing a definite disservice to Yoga, if we degrade the whole of it merely to a system of Physical Culture or therapeutics. But as long as we are ever emphasizing the fact that Yoga is principally a system of Physical Culture, there is no danger of our debasing the science.

Again when we see the imperfect attempts of Indian physical culturists to draw upon Yoga in developing their systems, we think it to be our duty to make a scientific attempt to evolve a Yogic system of Physical Culture and help our brethren that have already started the work. This attempt, if successful, will avoid much misunderstanding that prevails today, owing to a wrong use of Yogic exercises.

In formulating the scheme of Yogic Physical Culture we would fix upon the Yogic exercises irrespective of their spiritual value. Only their physical utility would be taken into account. The following exercises would constitute a self-contained system of Physical Culture.

Asanas: 1. Śīrṣāsana,
2. Sarvāṅgāsana,
3. Matsyāsana,
4. Halāsana,
5. Bhujaṅgāsana,
6. Śalabhāsana,
7. Dhanurāsana,
8. Ardha-Matsyendrāsana,
9. Paśchimatāna,
10. Mayūrāsana,
11. Śavāsana.

Bandha: Uḍḍiyāna

Mudrā: Yoga-Mudrā

Kriyās: 1. Nauli,
2. Kapālabhāti.

Prāṇāyāmas: 1. Ujjāyī,
2. Bhastrikā.

This is a complete scheme of Yogic Physical Culture. Having named the exercises we now proceed to see what an ideal system of Physical Culture should be, so that we shall be in a position to examine these exercises in the light of our ideal and understand their merits and demerits. During this examination we shall make a special effort to understand the underlying Yogic poses.

GLOSSARY

(**N.B.** – Reference to pages refer to the body of this handbook. Greek or Latin origin of words is given in the glossary. Saṅskṛta origin being given in the body of the handbook is omitted from here.)

(Grk. – Greek; Lat. – Latin; Skt. – Saṅskṛta)

A

ABDOMINAL AROTA	part of the arota situated in the abdomen, see aorta.
ABDOMINAL BREATHING	that type of respiration in which the abdominal movement is prominent.
ABDOMINAL RECTI	sing, *rectus* (Lat. rectus, straight), the two straight muscles of the abdomen crossing it vertically in the front.
ABDOMINAL VISCERA	sing, *viscus* (Lat. viscus, an entrail), the interior organs in the great cavity of the abdomen.
ABSORPTION	(Lat. *absorbeo* - *ab*, from *sorbeo*, to suck in), the process by which the circulatory system picks up nutritive elements from the digestive system.
ACCOMPLISHED POSE	Siddhāsana. (vide p. 59)
ACROMEGALY	a chronic disease characterized by the enlargement of the bones, and the soft parts of hands, feet and face.
ADENOIDS	(Grk. *aden*, a gland), masses of spongy tissue between the back of the nose and throat disturbing respiration.
ADRENALS	suprarenal capsules; endocrine structures situated above the kidneys.
AFFERENT	(Lat. *ad*, to and *Ferre*, to bring), conducting inwards or towards. See nerves.
AIR-CELLS	the extremely small circular bags in the substance of the lungs into which the inhaled air passes and across which it is diffused into the blood current.
ALIMENTARY CANAL	(Lat. *alimentum*, nourishment - alo, to nourish), food tube; the digestive tube.
ANABOLISM	constructive metabolism and assimilation. See assimilation and metabolism.

ANĀHATA - DHVANI	(Skt.), subtle sound heard by spiritually advancing students of Yoga.
ANAL - CONTRACTION	Mūla Bandha. (vide p. 56)
ANAL SPHINCTERS	the two sphincters situated an inch apart at the two ends of the anal canal which forms the last part of the colon. The lower and external sphincter constitutes the anus. See sphincter.
ANATOMY	(Grk. anatomē - ana, up and tome, a cutting), adj. anatomical, the science which deals with the structure of organized bodies.
ANTERIOR	(Lat. ante, before), more to the front.
ANTIPERISTALSIS	opposite of peristalsis (*q.v.*)- a wave-like contracting movement passing up the alimentary canal and pushing its contents backwards.
ANUS	(Lat. *anus*, the sitting part), adj. anal, the posterior opening of the digestive tube.
AORTA	(Grk. aeirō, I take up or carry), the great trunk of the arterial system issuing from the left side of the heart.
APPENDICITIS	(Lat. *appendo* - *ad*, to, and *pendo*, to hang; and itis, inflammation) inflammation of the appendix. See appendix.
APPENDIX	a small worm like organ attached to the cecum, varying from 2 to 20 cm. in length, the average being 9 cm. See cecum.
ARTERIALIZATION	the process of turning the venous into arterial blood.
ARTERIO-SCLEROSIS	(Grk. *skleros*, hard), chronic inflammation and consequent hardening of the arterial walls. See artery.
ARTERY	(Lat. *arteria*, Grk. *artēeria*), adj. arterial, one of the tubes through which the heart propels the blood to the different parts of the body.
ĀSANA	(Skt.) a Yogic pose.
ASSIMILATION	the process by which the cells pick up and utilize nutritive elements from the blood.

ASTHMA	(Grk. short drawn breath), a respiratory disorder characterized by difficult breathing.
ATMOSPHERIC PRESSURE	pressure exerted by the atmosphere and equal to that of a column of mercury about thirty inches or 760 mm. in height.
AUDITORY APPARATUS	(Lat. *audio*, I hear), organs of hearing.
AURICLES	(Lat. *auricula*, a little ear) the upper two chambers of the heart. (vide p. 15).
AUSPICIOUS POSE	Svastikāsana. (vide p. 61).
AUTONOMIC NERVOUS SYSTEM	a part of the nervous system that has independent functions. See nervous system.

B

BANDHA	(Skt.) a fixed arrangement of contracted muscles. (vide p. 54-55).
BASTI	(Skt.), the yogic method of flushing the colon. (vide p. 110, 125, 127)
BHASTRIKĀ	(Skt.), a variety of Prāṇāyāma characterized by incessant expiration followed by Kumbhaka.
BHRŪMADHYA-DṚṢṬI	(Skt.), the Frontal Gaze. This requires fixing one's eyes between the eyebrows. (vide p. 52)
BICEPS	(Lat. *bis*, twice, and caput, the head), the upper arm flexor, so called because of its having two heads or origins.
BILE	(Fr.), the brownish yellow fluid secreted by the liver.
BIOLOGY	(Grk. *bios*, life and *logos* a discourse), science of physical life, dealing with the structure, functions, origin and distribution of animals and plants.
BLADDER (Urinary)	the bag in which urine is stored up before it is discharged.
BLOOD PRESSURE	pressure exerted by the blood current upon the vessels through which it runs.
BLOOD - VESSELS	a flexible tube such as an artery or a vein that conveys the blood.

BOW POSE — Dhanurāsana. (vide p. 92).

BRAIN — the mass of nervous substance in the skull responsible for the expression of the various faculties of the mind.

BRONCHUS — (Grk. bronchos), pl. bronchi, adj. bronchial, one of the two branches into which the windpipe bifurcates in the chest. (vide p. 20)

C

CAPILLARY — (Lat. capillus, a hair), a minute blood-vessel connecting the smallest ramifications of the arteries with those of the veins.

CARBO - HYDRATES — (Lat. *carbo*, a coal, and Grk. *hydōr*, water), compounds of carbon with hydrogen and oxygen in proportion of form water, such as sugar and starches.

CARBON - DIOXIDE — carbonic acid gas; CO2.

CARDIAC — (Grk. kardia, the heart), of the heart.

CARDIAC ORIFICE — upper opening of the stomach, so called because of its proximity to the heart.
(vide p. 23)

CARTILAGE — (Lat. cartilago), adj. cartilaginous, gristle; a firm but elastic anatomical structure such as that forming the external ear or nose.

CATABOLISM — opposite of anabolism (*q.v.*) physiological disintegration; destructive metabolism. See anabolism and metabolism.

CELUM — (Lat. *caecus*, blind), the large blind pouch of the colon. See colon and also p. 23.

CELL — an ultimate element of organic structures.

CENTRAL ASPECT OF NAULI — Nauli-Madhyama. (vide p. 126)

CENTRAL NERVOUS SYSTEM — see cerebrospinal nervous system.

CEREBROSPINAL NERVOUS SYSTEM — that part of the nervous system which consists of the brain, the spinal cord and nerves issuing from them. See nervous system.

CERVICAL REGION	(Lat. *cervix*, the neck), that part of the vertebral column covering the neck.
CERVICAL VERTEBRAE	see vertebra.
CHIN - LOCK	Jālandhara-Bandha.(vide pp. 57, 76, 82, 100,101)
CIRCULATORY SYSTEM	the system consisting of organs responsible for the circulation of the blood; they are the heart, the arteries, the veins and the capillaries.
COBRA POSE	Bhujaṅgāsana. (vide p. 85, 86, 90)
COCCYX	adj. coccygeal, the lowermost part of the vertebral column. See vertebra.
COLON	(Grk. *kolon*, food), the large intestine.
CONGESTION	an abnormal accumulation of the blood in a part of the body.
CONSTIPATION	inability of the colon to throw out its fecal contents.
CONTRAINDICATED	forbidden because of the nature of the disease.
CRANIAL NERVES	the twelve pairs of nerves issuing from the cranium of the brain-pan. See nerves.
CRANIUM	(Grk. *kranion*, the skull), adj. cranial, the skull; bones enclosing the brain-pan.

D

DASKSHIṆA - NAULI	(Skt.), the Right Aspect of Nauli (vide p. 127)
DEAD POSE	Śavāsana. (vide p. 112)
DEVIATED NASAL SEPTUM	faulty position of the septum, that is the wall, partitioning the nasal cavities.
DHĀRAṆĀ	(Skt.) concentrating the mind upon one point. (vide p. 42, 131, 141)
DHYĀNA	(Skt.), continuous flow of the same ideation. (vide p. 42)
DIABETES	(Grk. *dia*, through, and *bainā*, I go on), disease characterized by habitual discharge of excessive urine with or without sugar.

DIAPHRAGM	(Grk. *diaphragma*, a partition), adj. diaphragmatic, the big muscle that forms the floor of the thorax partitioning it from the abdomen.
DIASTOLE	(Grk. *diastellō*, I open), applied to the dilatation of the cavities of the heart.
DIGESTIVE SYSTEM	this consists of the organs of digestion and elimination, such as the stomach, the small intestine, the colon, etc.
DORSAL REGION	(Lat. *dorsum*, the back), that part of the spine which support the back of the chest.
DṚṢṬI	(Skt.) a gaze.
DUCT	(Lat. *ductus*, a conducting), a tube to convey liquids.
DUCTLESS GLANDS	same as the endocrine glands, so called because their secretions are discharged into the blood current directly and not through any duct. Also see secretions.
DYSPEPSIA	(Grk. *dys*. ill, and *pepso*, I digest), adj. dyspeptic, indigestion.

E

EFFERENT	(Lat. *ex*, out and *ferre*, to bring), bringing away from. See nerves.
ENDOCRINE GLANDS	(Grk. *endon*, within and *krino*, separate out), glands which produce an internal secretion.
ENDOCRINE SYSTEM	organs anatomically and physiologically grouped together as having an internal secretion.
ENDOCRINOLOGY	(Grk. logos, a discourse), the study of the endocrine glands and their secretions.
EXTENSORS	muscles that stretch out the different parts of the body.

F

FAT	a greasy substance that deposits itself in the different tissues of animals.
FIBROUS TISSUE	tissue consisting of fibres, see tissue.
FINGER - LOCK	a lock formed by inserting the fingers of the opposite hands into one another (vide p. 67, 73, 82)

	FISH POSE	Matsyāsana. (vide p. 80)
	FLEXORS	muscles that bend the different parts of the body, such as the legs, the thighs, etc.
	FOOT-LOCK	a lock prepared by a particular arrangement of the legs. (vide p. 62, 73, 74, 75, 79, 117)
	FRACTURE	(Fr. from Lat. a breaking), breaking of bone or cartilage.
	FRENUM	(Lat.) a small ligament binding the tongue to the floor of the mouth.
	FRONTAL GAZE	Bhrūmadhya-Dṛṣṭi. (vide p. 52, 62, 100)
G	GALL - BLADDER	a pear-shaped sac in which the bile is stored up before it is thrown into the digestive tube. This sac is situated under the liver.
	GANGLIATED CORDS	nervous chains furnished with ganglia. See ganglion.
	GANGLION	(Grk.) pl. ganglia, a well-defined collection of nerve-cells and fibers forming a subordinate nerve centre.
	GASTRIC GLANDS	(Grk. gastēr, the stomach), glands situated in the mucous membrane of the stomach and pouring out the digestive secretion called gastric juice. Also called peptic glands because their secretion contains pepsin. See mucous membrane.
	GLAND	(Lat. glans, an acorn), an organ composed of cells secreting constituents of the blood.
	GONADS	(Grk. semen), sex glands, reproducing glands, namely, testes in the male and ovaries in the female.
	GOUT	disease with inflammation of smaller joints.
	GROIN	the depression between the belly and the thigh.
	GUPTĀSANA	(Skt.), same as Samāsana. (vide p. 63)
H	HALF LOCUST POSE	Ardha-Śalabhāsana. (vide p. 91)
	HALF MATSYENDRA POSE	Ardha-Matsyendrāsana. (vide p. 94)

HARD PALATE	the hard part of the roof of the mouth.
HAṬHA	(Skt.) Haṭhayoga; that system of Yoga which starts with the purification of the body as the first step towards spiritual perfection.
HEART	the muscular pump situated in the chest that keeps up the blood circulating in the body.
HEPATIC	(Grk. *hēepar* the liver), pertaining to the liver.
HERNIA	(Lat.), protrusion of the intestine through an abdominal opening.
HOISTED PADMĀSANA	Uttāitordhva Padmāsana. (vide p. 73)
HYDROCELE	(Grk. *hydōr*, water and *kēlē*, a tumour), collection of watery fluid around or near the testicle.

I

ILEO - CECAL VALVE	(Grk. *eilō*, I turn about, and Lat. *caecus*, blind), valve standing between the ileum and the cecum. (vide p. 23, 24, 27)
ILIAC BONES	(Lat. *iliacus*, from *ilia*, the groin), the two side bones in the lower portion of the abdomen.
IMPULSE	a sudden pushing force.
INTERCOSTAL	(Lat. *inter*, between, and *costa*, *a rib*), situated between the ribs.
INTERNAL SECRETION	see secretion.
INTESTINES	(Lat. *intestinum*, an *intestine*), bowels; two parts of the digestive tube lying between the stomach and the anus, called small and large. The small intestine measures twenty-two feet in length and is divided into three successive parts name duodenum, jejunum and ileum. The large intestine measuring five feet in length is also called the colon.
INTRA - ABDOMINAL	within the cavity of the abdomen.
INVERTED ACTION	Viparīta Karaṇī. (vide p. 122-123)
INVOLUNTARY MUSCLES	muscles which work independently of our will. See muscles.

	ISOLATION OF THE ABDOMINAL RECTI	Nauli Madhyama. (vide p. 125, 127)
J	JĀLANDHARA-BANDHA	(Skt.), the Chin-Lock, requiring the chin to be closely pressed against the chest. (vide p. 55, 60, 100)
	JIHVĀ - BANDHA	(Skt.), the Tongue - Lock. (vide p. 101, 120, 121, 136)
	JUGULAR NOTCH	(Lat. *jugulum* the throat) the depression below the throat and between the two collar-bones.
K	KAPĀLABHĀTI	(Skt.), one of the Shaṭ Kriyās consisting of a breathing exercise for the purification of the body. It is characterized by incessant expirations.
	KHECHARĪ	(Skt.), a Yogic exercise characterized by the prolongation of the tongue and by its being hidden behind the soft palate. This practice induced secretions which are claimed to be of a very great physiological value, and promotes deepest concentration helping the Yogin to go into Samadhi. (vide p. 120)
	KIDNEYS	the two abdominal organs which are mainly concerned in the excretion of urine.
	KRIYĀ	(Skt.), any Yogic exercise, especially any of the six cleansing processes. Also see Shat Kriyās.
	KUMBHAKA	(Skt.), a pause in the act of respiration. See Prāṇāyāma.
	KUṆḌALINĪ	(Skt.), the spiritual energy ordinarily locked up in an abdominal centre. (vide pp. 41, 108, 117, 119, 130, 131, 140, 141, 143)
	KUŚA	(Skt.), a kind of sacred grass.
	LARYNX	(Grk.), adj. laryngeal, the cavity forming the voice-box situated in the throat below the pharynx.
	LATERAL	(Lat. *lateralis*, from *latus*, *lateris* a side), situated on the side.
	LIGAMENT	(Lat. ligo, a tie), short band of fibrous tissue binding bones together.
	LION POSE	Siṃhāsana. (vide p. 99, 101)

LIVER	a large glandular organ situated below the right ribs that manufactures bile and purifies the venous blood.
LOCUST POSE	Śalabhāsana. (vide p. 90, 91, 93)
LOINS	region between the ribs and the hip-bones.
LOTUS POSE	Padmāsana. (vide p. 57-58)
LOWER EXTREMITIES	legs.
LUMBAR REGION	(Lat. *lumbi*, the loins), that part of the spine which is behind the abdomen. See loins.
LUMBOSACRAL REGION	that part of the spine which supports from behind the abdomen and the pelvis.
LUNGS	the two breathing organs situated in the chest.

M

MASSAGE	rubbing, kneading or otherwise manipulating the muscles and joints for stimulating their action.
MEDIASTINAL CAVITY	(Lat. *medius*, middle), the cavity that separates the two lungs in the chest.
MEMBRANE	adj. membranous, a thin sheet-like tissue lining such parts of our body as the mouth, the nose, etc.
MENOPAUSE	(Grk. *mēn*, a month), final cessation of the monthly flow of blood in the females.
MENSTRUATION	(Lat. *menstruus*, monthly), monthly flow of blood in the females.
METABOLISM	(Grk. *metabolē* change), the process of assimilation of food and its conversion into energy.
MOTOR NERVES	nerves designed to excite muscular activity. See nerves.
MUCOUS	n. mucus (Lat.), secreting a slimmy substance called mucus, such as covers our lips.
MUDRĀ	(Skt.) a symbol.
MŪLA - BANDHA	(Skt.), the Anal Contraction which requires vigorous contraction of the sphincters of the anus. (vide p. 56)

MUSCLE	(Fr.), any of the contractile fibrous bundles that chiefly constitute flesh. Muscles are of two kinds, the striped or striated and the smooth or unstriated. The striped muscles are voluntary and the smooth are involuntary. Involuntary muscles are not subject to the will. Voluntary muscles can be worked, as we wish.
MYXCEDEMA	a disease characterized by a deformed and idiotic face, slow speech and dull intellect.

N

NĀSĀGRA-DṚṢṬI	(Skt.), the Nasal Gaze. This requires fixing one's eyes upon the tip of one's nose. (vide p. 51)
NASAL CATARRH	(Grk. *kata*, down and *reō* I flow), inflammation of the nasal mucous membrane with a free discharge down the nose.
NASAL GAZE	Nāsāgra Dṛṣṭi (vide p. 51, 52, 62)
NAULI or NAULIKA	(Skt.), one of the Shaṭ Kriyās, being an abdominal exercise consisting of the rolling manipulations of the isolated recti. (vide p. 125-129, 133-134, 136-139, 146-150, 167)
NAULI -MADHYAMA	(Skt.), the Central Aspect of Nauli. (vide p. 126-127)
NERVE - CENTRE	(Lat. *nervus*, a *sinew*, *strength*, *vigour* and Grk. *kentron*, Lat. *centrum*, a prick or point), a group of nerve - cells functioning together.
NERVE IMPULSE	a sort of disturbance or push travelling across the nerves.
NERVES	fine thread-like or wire-like structures connecting the brain and the spinal cord with the different parts of the body. Messages running to and from across these wires are responsible for different sensations experienced by man and the various movements he makes. The nerves responsible for the muscular activity are called the motor or efferent nerves, whereas those that convey sensations from the ends to the different centres are called the sensory or afferent nerves. System consisting of these wire-like structures together with the brain and the spinal cord, manages all the voluntary and involuntary functions of the human body.

NERVOUS SYSTEM	see nerves. All the nerves put together, form the nervous system. It consists of two divisions, the central or cerebrospinal system and the autonomic system. The latter is subdivided into two parts, the parasympathetic and the sympathetic. The central nervous system mainly consists of the brain, twelve pairs of the cranial nerves, the spinal cord and thirty one pairs of the spinal nerves. The sympathetic is chiefly represented by two chains of ganglia-placed one on each side of the spinal column. The parasympathetic is found near the brain and the sacrum.
NETI	(Skt.), one of the Shaṭ Kriyās for cleansing the nasal passage by means of a wick inserted through the nose and extracted through the mouth or by means of water passed through the nose.
NEURASTHENIA	(Grk. *neuron*, a nerve), disease resulting from debility or exhaustion of nerve-centres.
NIYAMAS	(Skt.), see Yamas.

O

OESOPHAGUS	(Grk, *oisō*, I bear, and *phagein*, to eat), adj. oesophageal, the gullet, the canal extending from the throat to the stomach, some nine to ten inches in length, through which food and drink pass.
OLFACTORY NERVES	(Lat. *oleo*, I smell, and *facio*, I make), nerves responsible for the sense of smell.
OPTIC NERVES	(Grk.) *ōps*, the eye), nerves responsible for the sense of sight.
ORGANOTHERAPY	treatment of the diseases by the administration of animal organs or extracts thereof.
OVARIAN INSUFFICIENCY	incapacity of the ovaries to function properly. See ovaries.
OVARIES	(Medieval Lat. *Ovarium*, from Lat. *ovam*. an egg), the two reproductive glands of the females situated in the abdomen.

P

PADMĀSANA	(Skt.), the Lotus Pose. (vide p. 55, 57,58, 60, 62, 73, 75, 150)

PANCREAS	(Grk, *pan*, all, and *kreas*, flesh), a gland that is situated near the stomach and that provides a digestive secretion to the system.
PAN-PHYSICAL POSE	Sarvāṅgāsana. (vide p. 76-77)
PARASYMPATHETIC	see nervous system.
PARATHYROIDS	accessory thyroid glands, four in number, situated on the dorsal aspect of the thyroid.
PATHOLOGY	(Grk. *pathos* suffering, and *logos*, a discourse), science of structural and functional changes of organs caused by disease.
PEACOCK POSE	Mayūrāsana. (vide p. 110)
PELVIC LOOP	that part of the colon which lies in the pelvis and which opens into the rectum. See pelvis.
PELVIC POSE	Vajrāsana. (vide p. 102).
PELVIS	(Lat. a basin), adj. pelvic, the lowermost part of the abdominal cavity between the hip-bones.
PERINEUM	(Grk. *peristello* I involve), a wave-like contracting movement passing down the alimentary canal and propelling its contents.
PHARYNX	(Grk.), adj. pharyngeal, cavity with enclosing muscles and mucous membrane situated behind the nose, mouth and larynx. This cavity has openings which individually communicate with each of these organs.
PHYSIOLOGY	(Grk. *physis*, nature, and logos a discourse), science of the normal functions of living organism.
PINEAL	an endocrine gland situated behind the third ventricle of the brain.
PITUITARY	a ductlees gland situated in the upper region of the central nervous system.
PLEURAE	(Grk, *pleuron*, a rib), sing. pleura, the two serous membranes lining the thorax and enveloping the lungs.
PLOUGH POSE	Halāsana. (vide p. 81, 82, 88)

PLYPUS — (Grk. *polys*, many, and *pous*, a foot), tumour-like growth springing from a muscous surface as in the nose.

PORTAL CIRCULATION — (Lat. *porta*, a gate; particularly transverse fissure of the liver), circulation of the blood, from the digestive tract through the liver.

PORTAL VEIN — vein entering the liver.

POSTERIOR — adv. posteriorly, more to the back side.

POSTERIOR - STRETCHING POSE — Paśchimatāna. (vide p. 106)

PRĀṆĀYĀMA — (Skt.), adj. Prāṇāyāmic, the fourth item of Yogic curriculum; Yogic breath control; Kumbhaka. According to Svātmārāma Sūri there are eight varieties of Prāṇāyāma. They are: Sūryabhedana, Ujjāyī, Sītkārī, Śītalī, Bhastrikā, Bhrāmarī, Mūrcchā and Plāvini.

PRATYAHËRA — (Skt.), introversion of the mind.

PROTEINS — (Grk. *prōtos*, first), organic substances consisting of carbon, hydrogen nitrogen oxygen and sulphur.

PSYCHO - PHYSIOLOGICAL — (Grk. *psyche*, the soul and *physis*, nature), concerning the processes of mind and body.

PSYCHO - PHYSIOLOGY — science investigating the relation existing between psychology and physiology.

PTOSIS — (Grk. *ptōsis*, a fall), drooping down.

PUBIC BONES — (Lat. *pubis*, puberty), the bones just above the genitals.

PULMONARY, PULMONIC — (Lat. *pulmo*, a lung), of the lungs.

PULSE — throbbing of the artery felt in the wrist, etc.

PYLORIC ORIFICE — (Grk. *pylōros*, a gatekeeper, and Lat. *orificium*, the mouth), the lower opening of the stomach.

R

RAISING OF THE DIAPHRAGM — Uḍḍiyāna (vide p. 53)

RECTUM — (Lat. *rectus*, straight), that straight part of the colon which is situated just above the anus.

RECTUS	pl. recti, straight muscle.
REPLACING EXERCISE	an exercise which restores the abdominal organs to their proper places if they are displaced downwards.
RESPIRATORY SYSTEM	this consists of the organs of respiration, such as the lungs, the trachea, the bronchi, etc.
RHYTHMICAL BREATHING	harmonious succession of measured breaths smoothly flowing.
ROLLING MANIPULATION OF THE ABDOMINAL RECTI	Nauli. (vide p. 125)

S

SACRAL	n. sacrum, of the bone sacrum; triangular in shape this bone is formed of five united vertebrae and is wedged in between the two hip-bones. See vertebra.
SALIVARY GLANDS	(Lat. akin to Grk. *sialon* saliva), glands situated in the mouth which secrete saliva.
SAMĀDHI	(Skt.), the eighth stage in Yoga evolution wherein the individual either stands face to face with the infinite or becomes entirely merged into it.
SAMĀSANA	(Skt.) the Symmetrical Pose. (vide p. 63)
SCIATICA	(Grk. ischion the hip), pain in the sciatic nerve. See sciatic nerve.
SCIATIC NERVE	a nerve crossing the hip and thigh.
SCROTUM	(Lat.), the bag holding the testes.
SECRETION	juice manufactured by a gland to fulfil some useful physiological function. When this secretion is thrown directly into the blood current it is called internal; but when it is conducted through tubes called ducts the secretion is called external.
SEMINAL SACKS	the two small bags in the abdomen used for storing up the semen.
SENSORY NERVES	nerves that convey sensations from ends to the centres. See nerves.

SEPTUM	partition such as that between the two nostrils.
SEROUS MEMBRANE	(Lat. *serum*, whey), a smooth glistening membrane that secretes a lubricating fluid.
SHAT KRIYĀS	(Skt.), the six cleansing processes prescribed in Haṭha-Yoga for the purification of the body. They are: Dhauti, Basti, Neti, Trāṭaka, Nauli and Kapālabhāti.
SIDDHĀSANA	(Skt.), the Accomplished Pose. (vide p. 52, 55, 56, 59, 61, 103, 150)
SIṂHA - MUDRĀ	(Skt.), the Symbol of Lion. (vide p. 100, 120, 121, 136, 137)
SKELETON	adj. skeletal, the bony frame of the body.
SOFT PALATE	the soft part of the roof of the mouth.
SPHINCTER	(Grk. sphingō, I bind), muscular structure which surrounds a tube or an opening and closes the same by its contraction.
SPINAL CANAL	(Lat. spina, the spine), the canal formed by the different vertebrae standing above one another and holding the spinal cord inside it.
SPINAL COLUMN or SPINE	backbone. See vertebra.
SPINAL CORD	a thin rope-like nervous structure attached to the brain and lodged in the spinal canal.
SPINAL NERVES	see nervous system.
SPLEEN	(Lat. *splen*; Grk. *splēn*), one of the abdominal viscera situated to the left of the stomach.
STIMULUS	pl. stimuli, thing evoking functional reaction.
STOMACH	the principal organ of digestion, situated in the abdomen in continuation of the gullet.
SUPINE PELVIC POSE	Supta-Vajrāsana. (vide p. 104)
SUPRA - RENAL GLANDS or KIDNEY CAPSULES	see adrenals.
SVASTIKĀSANA	(Skt.), the Auspicious Pose. (vide p. 61-63)

SYMBOL OF LION	Siṃha-Mudrā. (vide p. 136)
SYMBOL OF YOGA	Yoga - Mudrā. (vide p. 118)
SYMMETRICAL POSE	Samāsana. (vide p. 63)
SYMPATHETIC	see nervous system.
SYSTOLE	(Grk. *systellō*, I contract), the contraction of the heart.

T

TACHYCARDIA	(Grk. *tachya*, quick, and *kar̩dia*, the heart), excessive rapidity of heart's action.
TESTES	sing, testis (lat.), the two reproductive glands of the males.
THERAPEUTICS, THERAPY	(Grk. *therapeuo*. I treat or cure), adj. therapeutical, science of healing.
THORAX	(Grk.), adj. thoracic, the chest.
THYROID	an endocrine gland situated in the neck.
TISSUE	(Fr. *tissu*, woven), distinct structure formed of similar cells and fibers.
TONGUE - LOCK	Jihvā - Bandha. (vide p. 101, 120, 123)
TONSILLITIS	inflammation of the tonsils. See tonsils.
TONSILS	(Lat. *tonsilla*), the two almond - like structures situated one on each side of the mouth just at the entrance of the throat.
TOPSYTURVY POSE	Śīrṣāsana. (vide p. 68, 70, 72)
TRACHEA	(Lat.), the principal air passage forming the windpipe. Some four inches in length, it starts in the throat and descends into the chest.
TRUNK	(Fr. *torne*, main body), human body without head and limbs.
TWISTED POSE	Vakrāsana. (vide p. 98)

U

UḌḌIYĀNA-BANDHA	(Skt.), the raising of the diaphragm. (vide p. 54)

UJJĀYĪ	(Skt.), a variety of Prāṇāyāma characterized by a smooth frictional sound through the throat, due to partial closure of the glottis in breathing.
UMBILICUS	(Lat.), the naval.
UPPER EXTREMITIES	arms.
UREA	(from the *ur* of *urine*), a soluble colourless chemical compound contained in urine.
URETERS	the two ducts through which urine passes from the kidneys to the bladder.
URETHRA	(Grk. ourēthra), the duct through which urine is discharged from the bladder.
URIC ACID	a particular acid found in urine.
URINARY SYSTEM	system consisting of the kidneys, the ureters, the bladder and the urethra, and responsible for the production and discharge of urine.
UTTHITORDHVA-PADMĀSANA	(Skt.), Hoisted Padmāsana (vide pp. 73, 75)

V

VAGUS NERVE	(Lat. *vagus*, wandering), the same as the pneumogastric nerve so called because of its wide distribution. This is the most extensive of the cranial nerves distributed to the lungs, the heart, the stomach, etc.
VAJROLĪ	(Skt.), sucking up of liquids through the urethra; control and sublimation of sex energy.
VĀMA NAULI	(Skt.), the Left Aspect of Nauli. (vide p. 127-128)
VARICOSE	(Lat. *varicosus*), swollen; knotted.
VEGETATIVE FUNCTIONS	plant-like processes in the human body such as the digestion, absorption, assimilation and others.
VEIN	adj. venous, one of the tubes which carry the blood from the different parts of the body to the heart.
VENE CAVA INFERIOR	vein conveying the blood from the lower part of the body to the heart.

	VENA CAVA SUPERIOR	vein conveying the blood from the upper part of the body to the heart.
	VENTRICLES	(Lat. *ventriculus*, diminutive of *venter*, the belly), the two lower cavities of the heart of cavities in the interior of the brain.
	VERTEBRA	(Lat. a joint), pl. vertebrae adj. vertebral, each of the thirty-three pieces which form the back-bone. The topmost seven are called the cervical, the next twelve the dorsal or the thoracic, the next five the lumbar, the next five the sacral and the last four the coccygeal.
	VERTEBRAL COLUMN	the backbone, See vertebra.
	VERTIGO	(Lat. *verto*, I turn), giddiness.
	VIPARĪTA KARAṆĪ	(Skt.), the Inverted Action. (vide p. 122, 123, 134, 136, 137, 139, 147, 154)
	VISCERA	(Lat.), adj. visceral, the interior organs in the great cavities of the body, especially in the abdomen.
	VISCEROPTOSIS	(Lat. *viscera*, pl. of *viscus*, an entrail, and Grk. *ptōsis*, a fall), downward displacement of the viscera.
	VOLUNTARY MUSCLES	muscles which are under the control of our will. See muscles.
X	X- RAYS	a kind of rays penetrating many substances impervious to ordinary light and thus extending the field of human vision; also called Roentgen rays after their discoverer.
Y	YAMAS & NIYAMAS	(Skt.), ten rules of the Yogic code of morality. (vide p. 41, 46-48, 162)
	YOGA	(Skt.), adj. Yogic, a system of exercises, physical or mental, which may begin with the purification of the body and which culminate in a stage wherein the individual soul becomes merged in to the infinite.
	YOGA - MUDRĀ	(Skt.), the Symbol of Yoga. (vide p. 96, 117-119, 146-148, 150, 152, 154, 157, 167)
	YOGA - SĀSTRA	(Skt.), logically systematized art and science of Yoga. See Yoga.

YOGIC PHYSICAL CULTURE	a systematic training of physiological functions through the exercises, prescribed in Yoga. See Yoga.
YOGIC THERAPEUTICS, YOGIC THERAPY	the science and art of healing by means of Yogic exercises. See Yoga.
YOGIN	(Skt.), a student of Yoga. See Yoga.

About Swami Kuvalayananda

Pioneer in Scientific Yoga

It is **Swami Kuvalayananda**, whose efforts are chiefly responsible for the worldwide spread of Yoga. It is due to his efforts that this ancient discipline of Yoga became more acceptable to modern mind, trained on scientific and rational guidelines. It is a fact that due to his scientific work, Yoga became more widely acceptable and accessible in the field of health & healing.

Swami Kuvalayananda (30 August 1883 – 18 April 1966) was a researcher and educator who is primarily known for his pioneering research into the scientific foundations of yoga. He started scientific research on yoga in 1920, and published the first scientific journal specifically devoted to studying yoga, Yoga Mīmāṁsā, in 1924. Most of his research took place at the Kaivalyadhama Health and Yoga Research Center which he founded in 1924. His influence on modern yoga has been "profound".

Early life

Swami Kuvalayananda was born Jagannatha Ganesa Gune in a traditional Karhade Brahmin family in the village Dhaboi in Gujarat state, India. At his matriculation in 1903, he was awarded the Jagannath Shankarsheth Saṅskṛta Scholarship to study at Baroda College where he graduated in 1910.

During his student days, he was influenced by political leaders like Sri Aurobindo, who was working as a young lecturer at the university, and Lokmanya Tilak's Indian Home Rule Movement. He realized the value of education, and this influenced him to help organize the Khandesh Education Society at Amalner, where ultimately he became the Principal of the National College, in 1916. The National College was closed down by the British Government in 1920 due to the spirit of Indian nationalism prevalent at the institution. From 1916 to 1923, he taught Indian culture studies to high school and college students.

Yoga Education

Kuvalayananda's first guru was Rajaratna Manikrao, a professor at the Jummadada Vyayamshala in Baroda. From 1907 to 1910, Manikrao trained Kuvalayananda in the Indian System of Physical Education which Kuvalayananda advocated throughout his life. As early as the 1930s, Kuvalayananda trained large groups of yoga teachers as a way to spread physical education in India.

In 1919, he met the Bengali yogin, Paramahamsa Madhavdasji, who had settled at Malsar, near Baroda, on the banks of the Narmada river. The insight into Yogic discipline, under the guidance of Madhavdasji, greatly influenced Kuvalayananda's career.

In 1920-21, he investigated the effects of some of the Yogic practices on the human body with the help of some of his students in a laboratory at Baroda Hospital. The idea of discovering the scientific basis behind these yogic processes became his life's work.

Yoga Mīmāṁsā

In 1924, Kuvalayananda founded the Kaivalyadhama Health and Yoga Research Center in Lonavla in order to provide a laboratory for his scientific study of Yoga. At the same time, he also started the first scientific journal devoted to scientific investigation into yoga, Yoga Mīmāṁsā.

The Saṅskṛta word Mīmāṁsā means "investigation." Yoga Mīmāṁsā, has been published quarterly every year since its founding and is scheduled to be indexed by EBSCO in 2012.

These experiments impressed some Western researchers who came to the Kaivalyadhama Health and Yoga Research Center to learn more. Dr. Josephine Rathbone, a professor of health and physical education, visited from Columbia University in 1928. K.T. Behanan, a doctoral candidate from Yale University, wrote his dissertation on yoga after visiting in the late 1930s. In 1957, the physicians Wenger, from the University of California, and Bagchi, from the University of Michigan, spent a month and a half working there. Research and collaboration continues to this day.

Later Years

In 1932, he opened the Mumbai branch of Kaivalyadhama at Santacruz. It was relocated to Marine Drive (Chowpatty) in 1936, and named the Ishvardas Chunnilal Yogic Health Center. Its mandate is the prevention and cure of various diseases through Yoga. In this same period, at Kanakesvara near Alibaug, a Kaivalyadhama Spiritual Center was inaugurated.

In 1943, he opened another branch of Kaivalyadhama in Rajkot, Saurashtra, with spiritual practices as its main focus.

In 1944 at Lonavla, the Kaivalyadhama Shriman Mādhava Yoga Mandir Samiti was founded to pursue scientific and literary research in Yoga

The Gordhandas Seksaria College of Yoga and Cultural Synthesis was established in 1951 at Lonavla to prepare young people spiritually and intellectually for selfless service to humanity.

In 1961, he opened the Srimati Amolak Devi Tirathram Gupta Yogic Hospital for the treatment of chronic functional disorders with the help of Yogic techniques.

Some of his pupils, like Padma Shri awardee, S. P. Nimbalkar, have become known yoga teachers in their own rights

kuvalaya

The Yogi

Who Started it all

About Kaivalyadhama

Virtually a university of Yoga, with many limbs.

Kaivalyadhama is not just one of the oldest Yoga Institutes in the world, but it is one of the most comprehensive. It doesn't just teach, but since 1924 it has carried out substantial and innovative studies into almost every aspect of Yoga's practice.

Swami Kuvalayananda founded Kaivalyadhama in 1924 after being guided and inspired by his Guru's philosophy that spirituality could uplift society. Above all his many skills, Swami Kuvalayananda was a great visionary who foresaw immense scope for the application of Yoga in all the spheres of life.

Kaivalyadhama's specific aim is to bring together traditional Yoga with modern science, as neither is thought to be complete without the other. Swami's view was that society had lost its way, and only a new and happy 'marriage' between the two disciplines could help to regenerate and build a better life for all.

Universal Spirit

From time immemorial, India's spirit has remained strong and vibrant with individuals such as Swami Kuvalayananda taking human form. The Institute's "raison d'etre" is to maintain this strength, and today Swami Maheshananda, as Chairman and Spiritual Guide of Kaivalyadhama, continues the succession with great charm and wisdom. Swami Maheshananda maintains a twice daily Havan (fire puja) practice to which all staff, students and visitors are welcome. The Swami is also available to all in the traditional way. Also, among the renowned visitors to Kaivalyadhama is the world renown Vedanta Acharya, Swami Anubhavananda. Classes are held on all aspects of Vedanta, especially the Bhagavad Gita.

Kaivalyadhama's Management

The Governing Body is the main policy making body. The advisory board which is chaired by former Supreme Court Judge, Justice B.N. Shrikrishna and comprises prominent professionals from fields related to the institutes activities, shapes how it does function both now and in the future.

Secretary General

Shri 0. P. Tiwari is Hon. Secretary of the Institute and responsible for executing decisions of the Governing Body. A disciple of Swami Kuvalayananda, he is one of the few sincere masters who teach the subtle techniques of Yoga in the classical way.

Classical Yoga education

Established in 1951 by Swami Kuvalayananda the Gordhandas Seksaria College of Yoga & Cultural Synthesis is an institute for the training of Yoga instructors. In fact, it has built a high international reputation for excellence, and students enroll from all parts of India and the world for yoga training. But the College's excellence is not just for training people as Yoga instructors. Substantial activities are also undertaken with the military, police and medical professionals, business executives and, not least, school teachers.

There are ten courses:

Special Two-track Yoga Certificate Course
Certificate Course in Yoga (6 weeks): Twice in a year
PG Diploma in Yoga Education (9 months)
PG Diploma in Yoga Therapy (1 year and 6 months)
21 days Certificate Course in Basic Understanding of Traditional Yogic Texts
Foundation Course in Yoga and Ayurveda (21 days)
Foundation Course in Yoga and Traditional Texts (21 days)
90 Hrs. Master Class for Yoga Teachers
Advanced Yoga Teachers' Training Course in (1 month)
B.A. – Yoga Philosophy (six semesters)
Online Yoga Teacher Training

The College is recognized by the Indian Government as an' Institute of Higher Learning. Yoga is taught by the College as a secular activity, but its two main paths: as a part of spiritual enquiry and as a science of health and healing, are both integrated within the teachings.

Pushing back Yoga's frontiers

The work of the Scientific Research Department falls primarily in two quantitative directions. First, cutting edge studies into the effect of Yoga practices, such as Āsanas, Kriyas and Prāṇāyāma, on diverse subjects as for example school children, yoga students, and police officers are carried out. Second, studies into the benefits of Yoga on various afflictions, such as obesity, diabetes, stress, and blindness. Several research projects are completed each year in the Department's fully equipped laboratories. These fall into six main categories: physiological, radiology, psychological, sports, biochemical, and neurological. With affiliation to the University of Pune, the Department mounts both M.Phil, and Ph.D. courses, while also collaborating with other Indian universities, as well as scientists in Europe and the USA.

Every Leaf a treasure

Yoga could not be complete without a learned body of writings, and it is the role of Kaivalyadhama's Philosophico Literary Research Department to provide what may be the world's most comprehensive archive specifically on Yoga.

The Department's first objective is to collect, analyze, disseminate, and protect ancient and modern works on Yoga. The basic work of the Department is to render traditional Yogic lore in a systematic and rational way so making it more accessible and understandable to all. Across the decades since 1924, textual discoveries and translations, and the publication of learned writings, have earned the Department much prestige. The library, which is open to all, contains over 31,000 titles and is itself a national treasure. There may be no greater Yoga resource than this anywhere in the world.

The Health Centre

The health centre at Kaivalyadhama has about 70 rooms and hosts over 3,000 people every year. People come for weekly packages consisting of yoga and relaxation, panchkarma ayurvedic therapy, naturopathy and massage therapy, yoga for obesity, beyond cancer, and the chronic cures retreat. The accommodation is spread across the campus, with simple clean rooms, attached toilets, air conditioning and vegetarian meals.

This happy place

Kaivalyadhama is at 120 km from Mumbai, and 60 km from Pune. Its height above sea level is 600 m, which means it is always refreshingly cooler than the coast area. Kaivalyadhama itself is spread across 180 acres of parkland and gardens and is full of trees, flowers, birds and butterflies, making it a beautifully open and serene place to visit. The staff and workers are a happy group and will give you a warm welcome whenever you may come.